Integrated Children's Services

Education at SAGE

SAGE is a leading international publisher of journals, books, and electronic media for academic, educational, and professional markets.

Our education publishing includes:

- accessible and comprehensive texts for aspiring education professionals and practitioners looking to further their careers through continuing professional development

- inspirational advice and guidance for the classroom

- authoritative state of the art reference from the leading authors in the field

Find out more at: **www.sagepub.co.uk/education**

Integrated Children's Services

John M. Davis

Los Angeles | London | New Delhi
Singapore | Washington DC

First published 2011

Apart from any fair dealing for the purposes of research
or private study, or criticism or review, as permitted
under the Copyright, Designs and Patents Act 1988,
this publication may be reproduced, stored or transmitted
in any form, or by any means, only with the prior
permission in writing of the publishers, or in the case
of reprographic reproduction, in accordance with the
terms of licences issued by the Copyright Licensing
Agency. Enquiries concerning reproduction outside
those terms should be sent to the publishers.

SAGE Publications Ltd
1 Oliver's Yard
55 City Road
London EC1Y 1SP

SAGE Publications Inc.
2455 Teller Road
Thousand Oaks, California 91320

SAGE Publications India Pvt Ltd
B 1/I 1 Mohan Cooperative Industrial Area
Mathura Road
New Delhi 110 044

SAGE Publications Asia-Pacific Pte Ltd
33 Pekin Street #02-01
Far East Square
Singapore 048763

Library of Congress Control Number: 2010940332

British Library Cataloguing in Publication data

A catalogue record for this book is available from the British Library

ISBN 978-1-84920-730-0
ISBN 978-1-84920-731-7 (pbk)

Typeset by C&M Digitals (P) Ltd, Chennai, India
Printed in Great Britain by CPI Antony Rowe, Chippenham, Wiltshire
Printed on paper from sustainable resources

Contents

About the Author

Dr John M. Davis is a Senior Lecturer in Childhood Studies at the University of Edinburgh. He has produced research reports, seminars, conferences, training materials and publications on a range of topics including:

- inclusion and interagency working
- participation in hospitals, mental health services, out of school clubs and respite care centres
- skills, training and blended learning in early years and children and family services
- equality issues in health, education, community, leisure and social services
- participatory research methods for working with children and adults.

Dr Davis's interests and activities in Childhood Studies come under the broad heading of Children and Social Justice. His research projects and publications cover theory, method and practice in the areas of disability, early years, ethnicity, education, health and social services. He has an international reputation for creating innovative projects that enable children and families to contribute to children's service development. His other books include: Tisdall, K., Davis, J.M. and Gallagher, M.J. (eds) (2009) *Research with Children and Young People* (London, SAGE); Tisdall, K., Davis, J.M., Hill, M. and Prout, A. (eds) (2006) *Children, Young People and Social Inclusion: Participation for What?* (London, Policy Press); and Davis, J.M. and Smith, M., *Working in Multiprofessional Contexts* (SAGE, forthcoming).

Acknowledgements

I would like to thank my family, Gill, Mel, Kate and Liam for their love and unwavering support. This book is about developing supportive environments that include emotional warmth, caring and listening – without such support from my colleagues, family and friends, this book would never have been written. In particular, the support provided by the children's grandparents Norma, Gladys and Peter has been invaluable, as has the support of my brother Mark and sister Jenny.

The information in this book has been drawn from my career working with children that first started as a sports coach at 12 years of age, and the thinking behind it first emerged whilst doing a PhD (completed in 1996). During that onerous task, I received scant supervision but a great deal of encouragement from fellow PhD students and teammates at Boroughmuir Rugby Club – specifically I would like to thank Anne Kerr, Eddie Donaghy, Gerry Dryburgh, Chris McFarlane, David Cockburn and Bill McNicoll. The book draws from work I have carried out across the UK. I would like to show my appreciation for the managers that commissioned the projects and the workers that gave me guidance throughout the projects. Eddie Still (formerly Lothian region), Bill Badham (at the Children's Society), Christine Mackay (Midlothian), Mike Jones/John Hogan (formerly of the Liverpool Bureau for Children and Young People) and Liam Cairns (at Investing in Children) were particularly inspiring.

The work has always been influenced by a range of academics and PhD students whom I have been supported by/supported over the years, including Erica Hayfield, Mairian Corker, Nick Watson, Marcus Readley, Sarah Cunningham-Burley, Kay Tisdall, Alan Prout, Malcolm Hill, John Swain, John Pinkerton, Pat Dolan, Tom Shakespear and Colin Barnes to name but a few. I have also received support from my work colleagues on the BA Childhood Practice Programme Team at the University of Edinburgh, including Lorna McNicoll, John Ravenscroft, Lynn McNair, Rowena Arshad and Jackie Bremner, and colleagues I have worked with on research projects, including Anne Hughes, Andy Hancock, Alan Bruce, Claire Whiting and Rana Syed. In particular, I have received support, counselling and extremely wise guidance from my friends: Mary Smith (who has taught me an immense amount about the connections between integrated concepts, structures and relationships), Stephen Farrier, who works tirelessly and Alan Bell, who along with the sadly lost Tom Conlon taught me more about fly fishing and relaxation than they will ever know.

Finally, to all family, friends and colleagues past and present, I hope this book honours your ideas and memories.

1

Introduction

Chapter Overview

This chapter outlines the key aims and rationale of this book. Before summarising the key arguments, you are encouraged to see the book as an academic and practical text that employs case studies and activities to enable you to get to grips with structures, concepts and relationships in integrated services.

An Integrated Text

Very few books take a truly integrated approach to writing about integrated children's services. In the main they are dominated by a specific subject bias e.g. either family work, community care, child protection, disability, early years, social work, etc. I have tried to overcome this problem by drawing from research and evaluation that I have undertaken in a range of services (health, education, early years, disability, family support and youth/community education). There are five case study chapters (Chapters 3 to 7), a chapter that defines integrated working (Chapter 2) and a chapter that draws together the different conceptual issues in the book (Chapter 8). You are encouraged to start with Chapter 2 as it sets out a straightforward literature review of writing that defines integrated working and should aid you to quickly get to grips with the different meanings of specific words (e.g. co-location, strengths-based, participatory, etc).

A Text that Draws from Practical Experience

Some of the books in this field tend to draw heavily from academic material/literature reviews, in contrast the chapters involving case studies in this book discuss the practical experience of staff, parents, children and young people before linking these experiences to academic ideas in a 'discussion' section. The book aspires to act as a sign-post to quality practice and to enable the reader to self-evaluate how they and their services measure up to a range of theoretical and practical ideas concerning integrated service delivery. The book is innovative in that it can be used in both teaching and practical contexts. For example, to enable students/practitioners and their managers/ colleagues to jointly consider the key issues confronting integrated children's services. The book draws from my experience of teaching students on the BA in Childhood Practice and the MSc in Childhood Studies at the University of Edinburgh. The Childhood Practice students take their degree part-time in the evening and work during the daytime. This means that the degree programme does not separate out academic from practical work. The two concepts are always in play. This differentiates the degree programme from dated approaches that separate out placement from academic work.

The activities in each chapter encourage the reader to pose questions, gather information and develop their practice in the places in which they work/ train. The book does not supply the answers to the questions posed in each chapter. You are expected to work those out with your colleagues, team members and/or managers. Though the case studies are drawn from Scotland and England, the book connects its ideas to issues in a range of countries (including Sweden, New Zealand, Ireland and Canada).

Content and Argument

Defining Integration: What are the Different Approaches? (Chapter 2) employs a range of authors to describe a variety of definitions of integrated working and suggests that there are a number of different starting points from which to attempt integrated working. It concludes that at its heart integrated working strives for some kind of jointness (Christie and Menmuir, 2005; Lloyd et al., 2001; Scott, 2006; Wilson and Pirrie, 2000). The chapter indicates that there is a continuum of integrated working including *co-operation* (at its simplest, information sharing), *collaboration* (processes of joint planning), *co-ordination* (more systematic than co-operation and involving shared goals), *merger* (the full integration/unification of services) (Cohen et al., 2004; Leathard, 2003b). The chapter stresses the need for integrated working to be based on clear professional practices, relationships, roles and responsibilities. It also makes a connection between the requirement for clarity and the need to develop 'harmonious relationships' (Bertram et al., 2002; Harker et al., 2004; Stone and Rixon, 2008). Interestingly the chapter does not connect harmony to political neutrality. It argues that discussions concerning conflict should be a central part of team meetings, forums and networks.

Some writers highlight the need for structural merger – others for conceptual unity built on strong relationships. This chapter tentatively begins the processes of analysing the meaning of these different perspectives and argues that the way integrated teams are set up effects their ability to overcome professional differences and build strong relationships (Anning et al., 2006; Glenny and Roaf, 2008; Tomlinson, 2003). The chapter critiques approaches that stereotype professionals and that lead to professional snobbery. The chapter highlights a tension between structure, concepts and relationships, indicating that some writers see relationship building as more important than structures (Anning et al., 2006; Gilbert and Bainbridge, 2003; Leathard, 2003b; Scott, 2006). Yet others argue that structures vary in their effectiveness over time and that good outcomes can be achieved from a range of models (Glenny and Roaf, 2008).

Chapter 2 introduces the concept of holistic 'strengths based' approaches that enable flexible services, consider the strengths of families/communities, mobilise support where people live, attend to issues of rights/equity and utilise informal support networks (Dolan, 2006, 2008; Gilligan, 1999, 2000).

'Strengths based' approaches are also connected to 'child centred' and 'client focused' perspectives that view children/families as the experts on their own lives (Foley, 2008; Leathard, 2003b; Rixon, 2008a). The chapter argues that we should move beyond approaches that work with children in isolation of their family and peer group and traditional deficit model approaches to children and families (Davis, 2007; Dolan and McGrath, 2006; Mayall, 2000; Tisdall et al., 2008). It calls for strong relationships to be built with both parents and children (Glenny and Roaf, 2008). In the main, the chapter considers the positive aspects of integrated working (subsequent chapters look deeper into the problems of integrated working). The chapter concludes by stating that there is no perfect way to do integrated working, that integrated working is fluid and that it requires critical engagement with parents/children concerning the pros and cons of specific approaches.

Chapter 3 – *Integrated Early Years Services: Co-location, Roles and Development* – considers issues concerning co-location, professional roles and qualifications/ training in early years children's services. It employs a case study (Davis and Hughes, 2005) from a Scottish local authority to discuss innovative structural, conceptual and workforce change. It questions the notion of a holistic pedagogical approach in early years because the concept comes from countries that do not have a tradition of integrated children's services and may overlook political issues. This chapter concludes that different professionals have varied experience of working face-to-face with children and parents in integrated childcare, education, health and social care services. Quality integrated early years provision is connected to the qualification levels of staff, however the chapter critiques the assumption that teachers should be managers and concludes that all staff (whatever their profession) need to make an equal contribution in integrated centres (Billingham and Barnes, 2009; Hawker, 2010). Structural and conceptual integration is linked to discussions concerning the development of a hybrid workforce. This chapter considers the idea that processes of integration require different professions to merge into a hybrid worker (pedagogue). It indicates that individuals in certain professional groupings (e.g. teaching and health visiting) are resistant to ideas of professional merger. Yet it also notes that many early years workers hold similar values and concepts and therefore that a professional merger in children's services may arise from a step-by-step process of relationship building during merged training routes, joint classes within qualifications, multi-professional CPD and the eventual development of a specific degree programme/qualification (e.g. similar to the BA Childhood Practice degree that has been developed in Scotland for managers/lead practitioners in early years, social work children/family centres, play and out-of-school provision).

The chapter concludes that there is conceptual resistance in Scotland to the structural merger of schooling with play, daycare, out of school and early years but that the new degree-level Childhood Practitioner (e.g. early years centre manager) may be a person who can strive to enable conceptual integration between different professionals. The standards for childhood practice are characterised as encompassing the best traditions of pedagogy that aspire to link theory, policy and practice (e.g. holistic approaches to the child's mind, emotions, creativity, history and social identity – Bruce, 2004; Cohen et al., 2004). It is suggested that the Childhood Practice standards may enable conceptual integration around more politically nuanced strengths based approaches (incorporating concepts of pedagogy, childhood theory, anti-discrimination and social justice). It is concluded that most professionals who work with children already have aspects of pedagogy in their practice, that the Childhood Practice degree could become a core aspect of the initial training of professionals who work with children in Scotland, that these processes could involve multi-disciplinary classes (or joint academic years) and that existing professionals should be required to carry out multi-disciplinary continuing professional development on key aspects of Childhood Practice. These conclusions lead to the suggestion that for such change to be effective it will need to be bottom up; prevent one professional grouping (e.g. teaching/social work) from dominating others; involve clear roles/targets; and involve a balance of staff providing daily, regular and targeted work.

Chapter 4 – *Integrated Children's Services and Ethnicity* – discusses the changing nature of early years services, it considers the strengths and weaknesses of early years services for black and minority ethnic families in a Scottish local authority area. It explains that an evaluation of early years services found that: only a small number of childcare providers employed staff specifically to work with black and minority ethnic children; black and minority ethnic parents and staff felt there was a need for more immediate and accessible interpreters for daily communication; a number of parents had no experience of participation in services; a large number of service providers made no overt effort to value and recognise diversity; and some black and minority ethnic parents were not happy with their provision (Davis and Hancock, 2007). The chapter concludes that greater sharing of resources (e.g. knowledge) should occur between those centres identified as high-quality service providers and those that have difficulties including children from linguistically and culturally diverse families. The activities in this chapter encourage you to consider the diverse nature of racism by adopting a community/strengths based approach to service provisions.

The chapter defines different types of racism: *cultural* (group behaviour); *structural* (resources, rewards, roles, status and power); *individual* (stereotypical views); *interpersonal* (harassment); and *institutional* (procedures, e.g. a culturally exclusive curriculum [Figueroa, 1993]). The chapter draws a distinction between writing that gives helpful advice on how to deal with issues of racism and writing that connects issues of anti-discrimination, equity and social justice to the ability of children's services to develop collaborative, capacity building, integrative and systematic approaches to working with communities. It also raises issues concerning the cultural appropriateness of European concepts of pedagogy, arguing that the westernised play ethos approach of pedagogy may not work for children who have culturally different starting points to those providing the services (Brooker, 2002, 2005; Clark and Waller, 2007; Smith et al., 2000) and that we should never assume that one country's approach, (e.g. that of Sweden) works in another (David et al., 2010).

The case study is compared to approaches in Canada that cross the boundaries between service provider and user (Ball and Sones, 2004; Moore et al., 2005) and contrasted with approaches in England that concentrate on academic 'school ready' criteria, westernised notions of 'skills development', and 'age appropriate' behaviour (e.g. Sylva et al., 2004). The chapter argues that we need to find ways to integrate community members into services through volunteering, training and employment and that we should engage with models of community governance. Professionals are asked to demonstrate multicultural competence; for example, the ability to speak about your feelings, respond to cultural variations concerning verbal/non-verbal queues, and display personal characteristics such as warmth, respect, genuineness, the ability to be honourable and the capacity to be practical, etc. (Moore et al., 2005). Family-centred approaches are defined as those that avoid imposing Eurocentric notions of assessment, involve families from the start of the development, promote local choice/decision-making, and strengthen family/community self help (Ball and Sones, 2004; Moore et al., 2005). You are encouraged to recognise the resources that immigrants bring with them and to consider how to utilise their values, skills and knowledge within processes of community development (Dolan, 2008). It is concluded that whatever your conceptual position, you need to develop approaches that put the participation of children, parents and community members at the centre of service development.

Chapter 5 – *Strategic Planning of Integrated Child and Adolescent Mental Health Services* – examines attempts by a local authority to develop a more strategic approach to children's and parents' involvement in integrated child and adolescent mental health services. The project involved qualitative work with children, young people and professionals. It also involved a review of previous reports – from local children's rights organisations, psychologists, universities and health services. The case study enables practitioners to consider the key issues of integrated child and adolescent mental health services. It discusses the development of a local mental health strategy, issues of prevalence, different professional approaches to assessment, participatory approaches and conceptual integration. It is argued that we need to question the way we assess children in relation to mental health because some adults fail to take account of children's own views. Practitioners need to question their personal assumptions and recognise the difference between their medical model presumptions and strengths based approaches (Davis, 2006; Davis and Watson, 2000; Davis et al., 2000). The chapter makes connections with Chapter 4, indicating that children and young people critique professionals who claim to take neutral approaches to 'treatment' and judge professionals on the basis of whether they care, are trustworthy, enable choice and take time to explain processes. The chapter indicates that a number of professionals identify with holistic approaches, promote the notion that services should be inclusive, and believe that children and young people should produce solutions for their own life issues. It concludes that different professionals need to be clearer about the different ways that they assess, characterise and treat children and young people, we need to consider the power relations within processes of consultation, participation, evaluation and review, and the development of holistic approaches must take account of local politics.

The chapter defines different assessment/treatment approaches to children and young people in child and adolescent mental health services. *Individualised approaches* highlight the individual child's pathology and judge children against normative criteria related to developmental age and stage. *Ecological models* (based on the work of Bronfenbrenner, 1989) consider the social context outside of the individual child (friends, school, neighbours, local services, national culture, government and the media). *Multi-agency approaches* aim to ensure that no one professional defines children's 'problems' or the solutions to their life issues, and politically nuanced *holistic models* (e.g. from the field of family therapy) challenge hierarchical approaches that assume that the medical professional knows best (assuming instead that service users are the expert on their own lives).

The chapter demonstrates the interconnectedness of the body to social places and the importance of understanding the role of social relations in different social locations (Dyck, 1999; Stables and Smith, 1999; Valentine, 1999). It highlights the importance of social as well as organisational aspects of mental health services. It concludes that integrated services have to confront conceptual differences and professional vested interests if parents, teachers, counsellors, psychologists and medical professionals are to move away from processes of labelling children and young people.

Chapter 6 – *Participation, Disabled Young People and Integrated Children's Services* – discusses the involvement of disabled young people in service development. It considers a case study of a 'Communications 2004' participation project that employed four disabled young people to ask children and young people what they wanted to change about local services and how they would like to engage with their local council (Davis and Hogan, 2004). The project found that children and young people wanted: disability awareness events; improved public transport; better transition to work; and greater inclusion in education, leisure, play and sport (Davis et al., 2006). It is argued that such projects are only worthwhile if they lead to real changes in the life conditions of disabled people (Davis, 2000; Davis and Hogan, 2004). The chapter demonstrates that the impact of the communications project was in the main positive but that it did not enable disabled children and young people to develop the type of sustained involvement discussed in relation to self-governance in Chapter 2. The project was partially successful in its specific aim: to build relationships between service providers and disabled young people. However, the project did not always enable the young people to reach the most senior of officials and so alter existing power relations, to effect speedy change. The chapter concludes that children and young people are aware of their lack of power, are frustrated by the limitations of participatory processes and that they wish to see a change in the power relations between adults and themselves.

The chapter highlights the difficulties of achieving participation in relation to disabled children and compares these difficulties to discussions concerning young carers that set parents' rights against children's rights. The chapter demonstrates a contradiction between rights based discourses and the notion that families and communities should be put at the centre of strengths based approaches. It indicates that the literature on young carers critiques individualised children's rights approaches because such approaches fail to acknowledge families as social rather than individual entities (Newman, 2002).

The chapter concludes that individual rights are useful when they enable legal recourse, but that they are closely related to deficit 'needs' based ideas concerning service provision. The chapter connects this idea to writers cited in Chapter 2 who argue that professionals should: develop flexible approaches (hold notions of minimum intervention), operate the concept of rights in a holistic way, attend to issues of social justice, and utilise informal support networks (Dolan, 2006, 2008). This perspective is also connected with the Canadian approaches discussed in Chapter 4 that argue for rights based, anti-discriminator, social justice perspectives that value all the actors who can support a child (e.g. peer group, family, community and professionals). As such, the chapter contrasts rights based discourses with strengths based approaches that require service providers to consider how provision can best address social issues (e.g. poverty, appropriate housing, access to transport), build relationships (e.g. overcome interpersonal discrimination) and develop sustained participation.

Chapter 7 – *Analysing Participation in Local Authorities: A Politically Nuanced Holistic Approach* – analyses the findings of two evaluations of a children's rights organisation, Investing in Children (IiC). Investing in Children runs a membership scheme for children's services who work in participatory ways, carries out specific projects/events, enables participatory processes, and develops participation strategies with children/young people and local authorities. The chapter indicates that IiC was strongly focused on children and young people's agendas. It enabled local authority, private and voluntary agencies to consider children and young people's life issues; and involved diverse children in inclusive projects while supporting children and young people's learning regarding disability/diversity issues. The chapter highlights the limitations of participatory processes arguing that children and young people are highly critical of the capacity of local services to respond to their life issues. It summarises the different criteria that people employ to define the benefits of participation, e.g. consumerist (produces services that are better value for money), pedagogical/developmental (teaches people), inclusive (connects different people), epistemological (enables us to produce better knowledge), political (it is democratic) and/or protective (listening makes children more likely to be safe). It also indicates that children and young people's criteria for successful participation is not always the same as professional perspectives and that both process and outcomes are important to children and young people that are involved in local authority decision-making.

This chapter demonstrates that participatory processes in integrated children's services can include a diverse range of children and young people while enabling children and young people to transform their life experiences and change local services. However, it also suggests that the diverse nature of children's services means that sustained strategic approaches are required that: consistently promote processes of dialogue; enable collective consideration of the effectiveness of integrated provision; and support integrated planning (to enable coherent, sustainable and structured approaches to participation). The chapter concludes that there is a need to balance out informal and formal approaches to participation, celebrate existing local knowledge-sharing networks/learning architecture, broaden the range of organisations/professionals involved in local collaboration; move beyond local vested interests; examine management hierarchies/rigid rules; and investigate the utility of decentralised structures. A central aspect of this conclusion is the belief that we can develop more culturally attuned services if we are more flexible and responsive to the needs of a wider range of children, parents and young people.

Chapter 8 – *Conceptual Integration in Children's Services* – synthesises the various ideas that have emerged from the case studies. It indicates that this book has attempted to compare different case studies to better understand the concepts, structures and relationships that support integrated children's services. It summarises the key conceptual issues that should underpin a strengths based approach to integrated children's services. In so doing it highlights a tension between 'child protection' (focusing on investigative approaches) and politically nuanced holistic provision. It suggests that the change in philosophy, culture and practice envisaged by integrated children's services policy has not been achieved because of the complex nature of children's services (Smith, 2007; Smith and Davis, 2010). It argues that many attempts to impose national frameworks overlook the politics of systems within local authorities and the need to instigate bottom-up service change (Smith, 2007; Smith and Davis, 2010).

The chapter briefly considers the holistic concept of pedagogy as a source of conceptual integration, however it argues that pedagogical approaches (particularly espoused in early years) tend to be applied ethnocentrically, are more a way of being (almost a belief system) than an actual concept, and are not well placed to consider and challenge the political context of deficit approaches. The chapter also considers the concept of social justice and community practice, arguing that there is a need to balance out concepts of individual and collective rights, that power should not be used as a gift and that individualised approaches to families are problematic (e.g. parenting programmes). The chapter concludes that whilst ecological models have their strengths (e.g. they encourage us to approach the child and family in a systemic way), they need to be connected with more fluid, politically complex, anti-hierarchical and participatory approaches (Davis, 2007; Dolan, 2008). Similarly, the concept of social capital is critiqued for creating 'social victims' and rarely engaging with contemporary ideas. The chapter examines post-structural and post-modern approaches that challenge traditional authority, promote the idea that identity is complex, fluid and ever changing, and emphasise the need for spaces of dialogue in contemporary integrated children's services. The chapter concludes that children, young people, communities and professionals have much to gain if we define integrated services as socially dynamic spaces within which practitioners are encouraged to constantly question their thoughts, practices and relationships.

The activities in the final chapter ask you to consider how your own ideas about children and families relate to both professional and personal concepts concerning play, socialisation, agency, inclusion, family support and the politics of welfare. The activities aim to demonstrate that theories shift over time, encourage you to develop complex approaches, concepts and relationships, and inspire you to consider how your conceptual starting points connect to ideas of social justice.

The chapters in this book encourage you to reduce the social space between yourself, children, families and communities, to consider your vested interests and embrace the complex identities of children, parents and other professionals. I hope you enjoy reading them as much as I enjoyed writing them and that you can see how privileged I have been to be able to work over many years with such capable children, young people, parents, communities and professionals.

Defining Integration: What are the Different Approaches?

Chapter Overview

This chapter draws from a range of authors to discuss a variety of definitions of integrated working. It discusses the structures, relationships, ideas and processes that underpin integrated working. It has five sections, entitled:

- Connecting Structures: Information, Policy, Processes and Resources
- Defining Integrated Working: Something More Connected or Joined Up
- Promoting Clarity: Professional Practices, Relationships, Roles and Responsibilities
- Sharing Understandings: Concepts, Identity and Specialism
- Achieving Participation: Diversity, Holism, Hierarchy, Self-Empowerment and Strengths Based Approaches

When reading these sections you are encouraged to consider your past, present and future workplaces and answer questions regarding your own/other people's practices. The chapter concludes that it is difficult to define integrated working because there is no set way to 'do it', that integrated working is an ongoing activity with constantly changing influences and that whatever your starting point, by building relationships on the basis of mutual critical engagement you will have an important role to play in supporting integrated approaches that engage more centrally with the perspectives of children and families.

Connecting Structures: Information, Policy, Processes and Resources

Many books on integrated working focus on the policy context that the author is troubled with (at the time of writing). Such books become dated because the policy context of children's services is constantly changing. In an attempt to overcome this problem, this text will very briefly summarise a number of aspirations that are found within policy documents concerning children's services before posing some key questions for you concerning the nature of the policies you encounter in your workplace. In so doing, this chapter encourages you to critically consider the underlying themes of policies rather than focus on any specific policy initiative. By not getting hung up on describing policy and concentrating on the connections between planning, thinking and practice, this text also aspires to be relevant to an audience wider than the UK.

Various policy documents in Scotland, Wales, England and Northern Ireland were published between 2000 and 2008 promoting integrated approaches to working with children (Jones and Leverett, 2008; Walker, 2008). Indeed, a number of authors suggest that recent policy developments in the UK follow in a long line of initiatives that have attempted to better combine preventative, proactive and protective services (Foley, 2008; Jack, 2006; Walker, 2008). These initiatives encompassed a number of key aims including:

- To consider the views of children and parents when planning services

- To shift from deficit approaches to strengths based and holistic approaches

- To offer services at the earliest possible stage

- To safeguard/protect children and enable them to live healthy lives free from abuse, victimisation and exploitation

- To address issues of conflict, diversity and inclusion

- To promote transition between services and to adulthood

- To improve information sharing and communication between professionals, families and children

- To enable learning, community involvement, environmental sustainability and economic well-being

- To move to an outcomes based approach involving more precise evaluation

- To move to a more joined-up way of working.

These policies placed a responsibility on a range of agencies to work together to monitor children, carry out timely joint assessments, liaise with parents, advocate for children, make decisions, refer cases on, and share information with other agencies (Walker, 2008).

Activity

Consider the bullet list below and the policy aims which you have identified as a result. How do they relate to your present workplace?

Throughout this book we will be questioning how such issues are played out in reality, who decides what these words mean in a local context and the barriers that exist which prevent children experiencing the benefits aspired to in such statements.

Write down:

- The local and national policy aims that most chime with how you want to do your job
- Any contradictions between the policies that govern your work and policies that create more problems than they solve
- The organisations that help you achieve the aims of your present work role
- The key people who support you to achieve those aims.

Feel free to create a chart or mind map to show this visually and keep this information so that you can look back on it as you work your way through this book. Also consider where you might want to take this information. For example, do you have a team meeting where your perspective can be raised? Is there a local, regional or national forum where you can influence how policy is developed?

Defining Integrated Working: Something More Connected or Joined Up

Many authors have tried to define integrated working. However, it is safe to say that it means different things to different people and that your views on its importance will depend on where your job is located. A number of writers suggest that it is not possible to give a formulaic description of integrated working but that at its heart is the idea of 'jointness'. Jointness is believed to occur when more than one agency works together in a *planned* and/or *formal* way or a single agency responds to the ideas/ decisions of others (Christie and Menmuir, 2005; Lloyd et al., 2001; Scott, 2006; Wilson and Pirrie, 2000). It may involve schools, health centres, play settings, children's centres, social work offices and community projects, or also educational psychologists, nurses, doctors, social workers, volunteers, faith group members, etc. (Fitzgerald and Kay, 2008; Glenny and Roaf, 2008; Leathard, 2003b; Rixon, 2008a; Walker, 2008). Similarly, it may involve more than one agency working with a young person, a family or a project (*multi-agency working*) or a range of services being provided by more than one discipline (*multi-disciplinary working*) (Malin and Morrow, 2007). Many writers discuss the nuances of intra (between different professionals in the same agency), inter (sharing) and trans (across) disciplinary/professional working (e.g. Fitzgerald and Kay, 2008). They suggest that it is important not to get too concerned with terminology as the same term may be applied in different ways by a variety of professionals, writers and academics (Fitzgerald and Kay, 2008).

It should not be assumed that integrated approaches are a new thing. For example, for many years in England voluntary and statutory agencies have collaborated on co-located campuses and in Scotland Community Schools have sought to bring services onto the one site and provide large-scale integrated approaches within youth strategies (Glenny and Roaf, 2008; Stone and Rixon, 2008). Similarly, it is argued that we should not view integration as a specific moment and that there is a continuum of integrated partnership approaches ranging from co-operation to integration (Frost, 2005; Stone and Rixon, 2008).

Co-operation

At its least complex, co-operation may simply take the form of smoother information sharing between agencies involved in the transitions of children between schools, services or life stages (Bertram et al., 2002; Frost, 2005; Leathard, 2003a; Stone and Rixon, 2008; Walker, 2008). Inter-agency communication may be formal and informal, written or oral and require agencies to work across traditional boundaries (Anning et al., 2006; Fitzgerald and Kay, 2008; Lloyd et al., 2001). Some writers highlight the benefits of employing a nested approach to communication where locations (e.g. schools) are connected to local hubs/groups that can input in local authority strategic management (Glenny and Roaf, 2008). Processes of information sharing are complex, not least because different agencies may have different approaches (Walker, 2008). Information can be shared where a child is at risk of significant harm, were there is reasonable cause to believe they are experiencing significant harm or where significant harm may be prevented (Walker, 2008). Confidential information can also be shared where consent has been given after clear explanation of an agency's policy (Walker, 2008).

At this level, services work towards consistent goals but maintain their independence – each striving to better achieve its own mission (Huxham and Macdonald, 1992; Stone and Rixon, 2008).

Collaboration

This can occur where services plan together (*joint planning*) with the aim of reducing duplication of services and shifting their efforts to address service gaps (Frost, 2005; Glenny and Roaf, 2008; Stone and Rixon, 2008). The *joint working* that may emerge from *joint planning* can be *concurrent* (e.g. involve staff from different services working with the same family at the same time) or it may be *sequential* (involve services working in series [Lloyd et al., 2001]). In either case there are believed to be added benefits from professionals from more than one agency working directly together (Leathard, 2003b; Lloyd et al., 2001). School based inter-agency meetings may involve *joint* planning, which reflects *joined-up* thinking (Lloyd et al., 2001). Some writers differentiate between horizontal collaboration (where children and families experience services concurrently) and vertical collaboration that facilitates a child or family's transition to the next level agency (Bertram et al., 2002). High-level collaboration occurs in processes of joint commissioning as agencies move towards greater co-ordination of effort and when participants work together to pursue a meta-mission while also pursuing their individual missions (Huxham and Macdonald, 1992; Leathard, 2003b). However, *collaboration* is less systematic than *co-ordination* because *collaboration* does not require the adoption of shared and agreed goals (Frost, 2005; Stone and Rixon, 2008).

Co-ordination

Very joined-up and deliberate, coordinated planning and working takes account of different agencies aims, goals, policies, practices and values (Frost, 2005; Lloyd et al., 2001; Stone and Rixon, 2008). *Co-ordination* can include agencies working together to develop joint thinking, practice or policy development (Lloyd et al., 2001). It can occur where there is no instantaneous service delivery in relation to a particular family, but where an organisation aims and plans to ensure that its own activities take into account those of others (Huxham and Macdonald, 1992). Examples of co-ordination have included *agency based* initiatives such as consortiums, panels, forums or locality groups that take account of different service boundaries (structures), planning cycles (procedures), funding/resources (finances), politics (status) and vested interests (professional domains/ self-interest) (Fitzgerald and Kay, 2008; Leathard, 2003b; Tomlinson, 2003; Walker, 2008). In an effort to overcome such problems, some forms of integration have moved to *process based* working that has strived to create a more unified approach (Leathard, 2003b).

Merger/Integration

Joined-up working may involve closer collaboration or co-ordination but not always necessarily the integration, unification and/or merging of services (Cohen et al., 2004; Leathard, 2003b). Full integration occurs when different services become one, where resources become shared/focused or where a unified one-stop shop model is achieved by amalgamating services (Bertram et al., 2002; Cohen et al., 2004; Frost, 2005; Gilbert and Bainbridge, 2003; Scott, 2006; Stone and Rixon, 2008; Walker, 2008). For example, a range of integrated centres emerged over time in early years services. These included single site centres, co-located campuses, integrated networks and multiple site integration (at more of a distance). Here, connected services inhabit the same or several locations and offer either specialist services or a range of services (including outreach) (Bertram et al., 2002; Glenny and Roaf, 2008; Walker, 2008). The role of one-stop shops cannot only be to introduce children and parents to a wide range of support that can address immediate concerns but must also enable reciprocity where people over time can become a resource within the community to support others (Broadhead et al., 2008; Dolan, 2008). Sometimes, in the most innovative integrated approaches the notion of community spreads across countries and continents (Broadhead et al., 2008). In other cases these approaches build on long-held community traditions (Dolan, 2008).

Process based integrated working involves organised merger, whole systems approaches, service level agreements, local flexibility, teamwork, joint learning and/or liaison (Fitzgerald and Kay, 2008; Leathard, 2003b). It is synergistic and non-conventional (Christie and Menmuir, 2005; Roaf, 2002; Scott, 2006; Wilson and Pirrie, 2000). It is something bigger than the objectives of a group of organisations (Huxham and Macdonald, 1992). Such transformational developments have required courage, determination, resources and commitment in order to achieve a cohesive web of support for children and families (Bertram et al., 2002; Leathard, 2003b). At the centre of this shift is the notion that there is something extra gained from building strong trustful professional relationships, be that through merger, coalition/federation, discrete model or a professional partnership (Bertram et al., 2002; Leathard, 2003a; Stone and Rixon, 2008; Walker, 2008).

The majority of professionals in children's services will work in interdisciplinary teams at some point in their careers (Fitzgerald and Kay, 2008). *Process based* approaches raise issues for different professionals depending on whether they feel part of the team, are conscripted, experience status issues, consider themselves a core or peripheral member, have support for professional ongoing development/specialist skills retention and experience in internal/ external line management (Anning et al., 2006; Harker et al., 2004; Stone and Rixon, 2008). The processes through which work activities are deployed, the location of activities, the sharing of protocols, the agreeing of strategic objectives, the status/responsibility of a role, the nature of staff contracts (full/ part-time, seconded/permanent, new/traditional service, bolt-on service, etc.), the ability to commit to team/shared decision making, clear lines of accountability, etc., are all factors that have to be worked through in more integrated approaches (Anning et al., 2006; Glenny and Roaf, 2008; Harker et al., 2004; Stone and Rixon, 2008; Tomlinson, 2003). Some writers highlight the importance of recognising the politics of how integrated approaches are developed. For example, there may be differences between where policy texts/agreements are produced and where practice occurs (Jones and Leverett, 2008; Smith and Davis, 2010).

Activity

Consider the issues in this section and return to your notes from the previous activity. How integrated is your workplace (or settings where you have been on placement)? Does it involve merged services or single services? Do you (or people like you) only interact with other services when families are in crisis? Do other services share information with you, jointly plan within forums, and deliver services together or on the same site? How could your approach be improved? For example, if you do not have much knowledge of integrated working could you identify and attend a local forum? Alternatively, could you identify sets of professionals to come to your own team meetings? If you want to move to more integrated approaches, where do you have to take this aspiration – who do you need to speak to? If you are already involved in an integrated approach, is there clarity regarding aims, roles, protocols, etc.? If you are a student, you may want to consider the places you have previously worked with children or experienced services yourself.

Promoting Clarity: Professional Practices, Relationships, Roles and Responsibilities

Process based approaches to integrated working involve collaboration (for example in teams) that seeks to achieve a co-ordinated, synchronised model that is built on 'harmonious relationships' (Bertram et al., 2002; Harker et al., 2004; Stone and Rixon, 2008). Some authors highlight the process through which teams can be built, for example through joint training, appraisal, recognition/respect of diverse professional identities, and involvement of different personality types (e.g. dependable contributors, good communicators, goals focused collaborators and question focused challengers) (Leathard, 2003b; Tomlinson, 2003). Many authors suggest that leadership/management that builds inter-professional respect and trust is a central aspect of successful integration (Anning et al., 2006; Bertram et al., 2002; Frost, 2005; Harker et al., 2004; Leathard, 2003b; Stone and Rixon, 2008). They suggest that good management involves regular meetings, praising contributions, the development of group coping strategies, the ability to enable dialogue (especially concerning disputes), informed choice, equality of access to information, strong avenues of communication, and anti-discriminatory practice (Anning et al., 2006; Bertram et al., 2002; Walker, 2008). It is concluded that the way integrated teams are organised/managed affects their ability to overcome professional differences by building strong relationships and that full strategic and operational commitments are required if effective partnerships are to flourish (Anning et al., 2006; Glenny and Roaf, 2008; Tomlinson, 2003). In particular, it is suggested that an individual needs to 'mind the system' to ensure the network of relationships are sustained (e.g. through the development of communication structures, monitoring of task completion, and reminding people of the history of the development) (Glenny and Roaf, 2008).

Considering Professional Groups?

Many authors suggest that professional groups can be defined by the way they self-regulate and respond to the people who use their services (Anning et al., 2006; Frost, 2005). They are characterised by social status, hierarchies, sets of ethics, processes of accountability/regulation, the requirement to possess specific qualifications, the privileging of particular bodies of knowledge, definite rates of pay, and the manipulation of power relations towards their own vested interests (Aldridge and Evetts, 2003; Anning et al., 2006; Banks, 1998a & b; Freeman, 1996; Macdonald, 1995; Rugland, 1993; Sims et al., 1993; Tomlinson, 2003; Walker, 2008).

However, some authors suggest the concept of professional groupings is problematic in contemporary society because it tends to overplay the notion of professional identity and that it should not be considered an absolute definition of who a person is (Anning et al., 2006; Friedson, 1983; Frost, 2001; Larson, 1997; Leathard, 2003a). Indeed a central aspect of integrated working may be the facilitation of transition to new professional identities (Anning et al., 2006). This is not aided by processes of professional stereotyping that often involve (sometimes quite calculatedly) the downplaying of the importance of innovative integrated working roles (Smith and Davis, 2010; Walker, 2008). Later chapters will discuss how strong relationships can be built when professional stereotypes are broken down and professional snobbery is challenged. In particular, this book will challenge the notion that innovative degree-level (e.g. family worker, early years/Sure Start manager, welfare worker, etc.) and non-degree-level practitioners (assistant family worker, early years practitioner, community worker, social care assistant) are somehow semi-, para or lesser professionals. It is important that we do not create stereotypes about different professionals, for example that social workers are always late, teachers are lucky to get long holidays or nurses are angels (Walker, 2008). It is important here to realise that not all social workers, teachers and nurses are the same and that very often if these workers are not aiding the processes of integration, it may be because of personal and professional pressures that they are experiencing and not because they are somehow 'bad' people.

Building Strong Professional Relationships

Many authors stress the importance of building relationships by working or learning together. They argue that joint training can help workers from different disciplines to develop common skills, form new relationships and create a common language (Leathard, 2003a; Marks, 1994; Milne, 2005; Scott, 2006; Stone and Rixon, 2008). Similarly, strong relationships can be developed within processes that encourage different professionals to identify a common challenge, take systematic approaches, share objectives and evolve solutions (Fitzgerald and Kay, 2008; Glenny and Roaf, 2008; Milne, 2005; Scott, 2006; Walker, 2008). Some writers argue that what matters more in integrated approaches is that professionals work and learn together, show awareness of where power is located, and identify clear goals rather than whether they are working between, within or across agencies (Anning et al., 2006; Gilbert and Bainbridge, 2003; Leathard, 2003b; Scott, 2006). At the heart of this way of working is the idea that integrated working flourishes in conditions where workers enjoy simultaneous face-to-face encounters, have opportunities to utilise humour, can develop systems for analysing the information from meetings, experience joint ownership of working spaces, are confident to share/make explicit their knowledge, recognise each other's skills and have space/time to review joint activities/issues of conflict (Anning et al., 2006; Glenny and Roaf, 2008; Reeves and Freeth, 2003; Scott, 2006; Walker, 2008). In particular, there may be a need to consider role terminology and whether team members are willing to move beyond titles such as social worker, teacher, nurse, etc. to consider themselves part of a new team (e.g. Child Development Team/Integrated Working Team) (Anning et al., 2006). The process of building strong professional relationships is not easy and may involve particular trauma for staff who have their titles changed, feel they are being deskilled, have to hand over their duties to other staff and/or have to train up staff to take on some of their own roles (see e.g. social workers: Stone and Rixon, 2008; Walker, 2008; teachers and speech therapists: Anning et al., 2006). It may also require managers to share authority, become aware of the strengths of the people they work with, and be sensitive to staff vulnerabilities, yet avoid infantilising staff (Anning et al., 2006).

However, it is argued that there are strong benefits concerning self-esteem to be gained by staff who successfully develop/transform their roles and are able to reflect on the everyday experience of such processes (Anning et al., 2006). The relationships in integrated children's services are characterised by their fluid nature and it is argued that tensions should be seen as inevitable and attempts to overcome conflict should make a virtue out of the fact that there are professional differences (Anning et al., 2006). Processes of sharing different personal and professional understandings can place at their centre an attempt to reflexively examine the impact of the different concepts that professionals hold (Anning et al., 2006; Davis, 1998). The start of this chapter defined integration as a process of aligning professionals through structural change but some authors argue that structures vary in their effectiveness over time and that good outcomes can be achieved from a range of models (Glenny and Roaf, 2008). This section suggests that this may be because integration, though benefiting from structural cohesion, is also a process where relationships are built that result in conceptual unity (Cohen et al., 2004; Scott, 2006).

Activity

It is particularly important for trainees and students that are currently studying for degrees to have a reality check regarding their attitudes to staff they encounter who work at practitioner level (e.g. in Scotland staff who are qualified to HNC level or equivalent). There is nothing more problematic for integrated working than the assumption that a staff member is somehow lesser because they do not possess a degree. Very often these staff members spend the most time with children and have the most in-depth and everyday knowledge regarding the children's wishes and aspirations.

Pause for a moment and reflect on your attitudes towards different staff members. If you are a leader/manager, what do you do in your workplace to demonstrate that discrimination towards non-degree-level professionals is unacceptable – do you hold team meetings that exclude specific staff members? Do the non-degree-level staff that know a child or family best actually attend the meetings that discuss their services? How do you ensure that there are clear avenues of communication so that the ideas of all staff are considered in the workplace? If you are a staff member or a student on placement, how hierarchical is your workplace? Do some colleagues get referred to by their first names whereas others are referred to by their titles? How equitable are the working practices? Are specific staff excused from attending meetings/carrying out integrated working tasks because of their professional status? Do you have the confidence to share your conceptual differences with other professionals and to question their perspectives?

Sharing Understandings: Concepts, Identity and Specialism

Service integration can be structural (involving changes in department responsibility, funding, staffing, regulation) and conceptual (involving the development of shared principles, values, identities, approaches to practice, understandings regarding children, etc.) (Cohen et al., 2004). Professional boundaries can be blurred, greater tolerance of other disciplines can emerge and an ideological shift can be created by conceptual integration that enables a shared ideology to come about that is based on shared principles and values (Leathard, 2003b; Scott, 2006; Wilson and Pirrie, 2000). The importance of achieving conceptual unity has been related to the need to provide service users with consistent rather than contradictory advice (Glenny and Roaf, 2008).

Some writers suggest that moves to integrated working have been flawed where new structures, strategies and programmes have been traditionally driven in a top-down way by government or one specific agency (Cohen et al., 2004; Glenny and Roaf, 2008). They argue that more consideration should be given to the way that different group/professional principles, traditions, practices, concepts and cultures impact on integrated working initiatives (Cohen et al., 2004; Glenny and Roaf, 2008; Walker, 2008). Indeed, top-down approaches overlook the need to stimulate integrated working by creating the conditions that provoke thinking, including attending workshops that enable professionals to develop tools for analysing change, reading books/articles and visiting other services (Anning et al., 2006; Cohen et al., 2004). Alternatively, a more coherent approach promotes the notion that integrated working should enable professionals to individually and collectively work through the collision that occurs when different specialisms interact (Stone and Rixon, 2008).

Holistic Working?

A notion emerges that integrated working requires different professionals to develop a holistic theoretical, professional and personal position (Leathard, 2003b; Seebohm, 1989). 'Seamless transition' is thought to emerge through co-operation, collaboration alignment and the consideration of holism (e.g. connected thinking and ideology) (Bertram et al., 2002). Processes of integration are described by outputs, shared ideologies and critical co-operation towards a mutually understood end (Scott, 2006). Central to these processes is the concept of dialogue and the development of social, cultural and discursive places where children, parents and professionals can work towards more integrated solutions (Moss and Petrie, 2002).

However, this raises tensions concerning whether the logical conclusion to integrated approaches is a single children's services worker (which some refer to as a pedagogue); whether the balancing of different professional groupings with some core understandings is a more effective approach; or whether full partnership working is a utopia (see Cohen et al., 2004; Rixon, 2008a; Stone and Rixon, 2008; Walker, 2008). Some writers suggest that integrated working seeks to balance the influence of different professions and their concepts. That it is additive and multiplicative. That each agent brings their own specialism, no one specialism has overall control and a combined integration of efforts achieves more than the parts would achieve on their own (Anning et al., 2006; Leathard, 2003a; Scott, 2006).

This issue will be more fully discussed in future chapters in relation to politically nuanced working, however it is important to indicate here that holistic approaches are not easy to achieve and that the different theories that underpin professional working in children's services are not necessarily compatible or easily amalgamated (Anning et al., 2006). This may be particularly the case in rural settings (Glenny and Roaf, 2008).

 Activity

> Consider your own personal perspectives of childhood. How do these influence the way you work? Do other professionals (or the people taking your course) hold similar views? How do your personal ideas connect to different professional concepts? How open are you to working with other professionals, developing shared ideologies and/or taking on new ideas?

Achieving Participation: Diversity, Holism, Hierarchy, Self-Empowerment and Strengths Based Approaches

Holistic inter-agency practices are described as programmes that work towards specific goals and reduce the proportion of children referred through child protection (Roaf, 2002; Walker, 2008). There is an attempt to intervene as early as possible in children's lives, to broaden out those who might experience services and to avoid approaches that involve service rationing (Aldgate and Tunstill, 1995; Glenny and Roaf, 2008; McGhee and Waterhouse, 2002; Tisdall, 1997; Walker, 2008). The aim is to overcome approaches that limit service provision to those in acute need of child protection measures by supporting families earlier and quicker (Jeffrey, 2003; Smith and Davis, 2010). This requires the balancing of universal, targeted, developmental, compensatory and protective services (Gilligan, 2000; Glenny and Roaf, 2008). For example, some writers recommend that services are mapped to avoid us re-inventing the wheel or that an audit of community assets (physical, human, participatory and governmental) is carried out to enable planning for a positive future (Dolan, 2008; Glenny and Roaf, 2008). They also recognised that early intervention may be difficult because many workers do not feel they have time to be involved in non-critical cases and families themselves may not welcome what they see as intrusive approaches (Glenny and Roaf, 2008).

Moving to Strengths Based Approaches

Some writers have sought to emphasise the 'principles' that should under-pin the development of new approaches to working with children and families. They suggest that professionals should aim to develop flexible services that are underpinned by a notion of minimum intervention, consider the strengths of families/communities, attend to issues of rights/equity and utilise informal support networks (Dolan, 2006, 2008). At the centre of these new ways of working is the idea that professionals should mobilise support where children live their lives (e.g. school, peer group, wider family) (Gilligan, 1999, 2000).

Many holistic approaches are based on the work of Bronfenbrenner (1989) that recognises issues outside of the individual child. Bronfenbrenner (1989) located the child within a series of rings (or Russian Dolls) of influence (David et al., 2010; Dolan, 2008). This enables writers on integrated services to suggest that all aspects of children's lives are inextricably linked. A number of authors use child development theory to demonstrate that children's overall development is influenced by a range of factors in the environment they live in, for example family relationships, school, wider community/society (Aldgate, 2006; Fawcett, 2000; Stone and Rixon, 2008).

Children's Participation in Integrated Services

The ecological perspective enables psychologists to move away from traditional approaches that have tended to label children and families as deficit towards approaches that adopt a 'child centred' perspective. Later chapters will critique the ecological approach, however it is useful here to consider how it enables professionals within integrated services to become more 'client focused' (Leathard, 2003b) and to start their analysis/assessment with the experiences of children and families, view children as agents with a wealth of experience/views and enable children's ongoing participation in decisions about service provision (Rixon, 2008b). This requires adults to challenge traditional assumptions about children and to avoid tokenistic approaches (Davis, 2007; Mayall, 2000; Tisdall et al., 2008). It requires strong relationships to be built with both parents and children (Glenny and Roaf, 2008). The involvement of service users in integrated service development is promoted by a number of authors (Foley, 2008;

Leathard, 2003b). Some writers highlight the importance of not working with children in isolation and of including parents and peer groups in integrated family work (Dolan and McGrath, 2006). Equally, concerns have been raised about integrated approaches, for example Sure Start initiatives that focus on the learning of the child are thought to have had more limited impact on maternal mental health, helping parents cope with stressful life events and/or issues of welfare dependency (Fergusson et al., 2006; Rutter, 2007). It is suggested that children and parents particularly value processes where adults build flexible relationships and that processes of participation enable such bonds to be built (Davis, 2007; Dolan, 2008).

Participation is not easy and issues of funding, time, bureaucracy, leadership, staff training/experience, inaccessible language, out of the way locations, internal governance, and so forth, all create barriers to listening to children (Badham, 2000; Cairns, 2006; Davis, 2007; Davis and Hogan, 2004). This issue will be returned to as we progress through the book and try to understand children and parents' own perspectives of integrated working.

Conclusion

This chapter has employed a range of authors to describe a variety of definitions of integrated working. It has suggested that there are a number of different starting points from which to attempt integrated working. Some writers highlight the need for structural merger, others for conceptual unity built on strong relationships. This chapter tentatively began the processes of analysing the meaning of these different perspectives. It highlighted the call for 'strengths based' approaches and conceptual integration. It discussed issues of professional hierarchy and described the request for clear roles, objectives and procedures. In the main, this chapter highlighted writing that promotes integrated working as a means of improving the way we work with children and parents. As we work through this book, we will look more at the problems of integrated working and begin to analyse more deeply the perspectives outlined above. It is important for you as the reader to realise that there is no perfect way to do integrated working (it is a contested area), that integrated working is fluid and constantly changing and that it requires different professionals to build relationships to enable critical engagement with parents and children concerning the pros and cons of specific approaches.

3

Integrated Early Years Services: Co-location, Roles and Development

Chapter Overview

This chapter discusses issues concerning co-location, professional roles and qualifications/training in early years children's services. It employs a case study from a Scottish local authority to highlight the tensions between innovative structures, conceptual change and workforce development (Davis and Hughes, 2005). It illustrates different perspectives on integrated working and culminates in a discussion that considers a number of key questions:

- Can structural change and a holistic pedagogical approach enable systematic integration of care and education services?
- What are the problems with linking early years and play with schooling?
- What are the barriers to developing a hybrid pedagogue role and what might an integrated early years team look like?

Students/practitioners are asked to consider their position within children's services, the autonomy of their role and their workplace responsibilities. Specific barriers to integrated early education are identified with the aim of forewarning students about the pitfalls they might find in their evolving work roles. This chapter concludes that different professionals are better/worse placed to respond to attempts to integrate childcare, education, health and social care services.

The following case study involves extracts from a summary of a project carried out by the author and Anne Hughes of Strathclyde University. It is included with the kind permission of Anne Hughes.

Davis and Hughes (2005) carried out research into competencies, qualifications and skills of staff in early years services. They:

- audited existing staff in early years in relation to current deployment, required competencies and levels and range of qualifications held against these competencies

- assessed the likely impact of the development of integrated services on the competency requirements and therefore the deployment and use of staff

- assessed the possibilities for the creation of career progression opportunities for the staff against a recognised training and qualifications structure and in the context of the Scottish Credit and Qualifications Framework (SCQF).

Integrated Early Years Services, Roles, Specialism and Qualifications

Common Roles

Davis and Hughes (2005) found that workers identified a number of common or generic work roles: developing and observing children's interest, knowledge and skills (80.1%); welcoming and caring for children (78.5%); assessing and reporting on children's progress (75.4%); leading group activities (60.2%); and working with parents to develop parenting and educational skills (41.4%).

In relation to the delivery of the outcomes required of integrated early years services, the workforce felt confident in their knowledge and skills in 'Children's Learning and Development'. About half felt that they had skills in 'Reducing Risk, Improving Parenting Skills and Confidence Levels' and 'Enhancing Children's and Families' Health and Well-Being Level'.

Some staff showed a willingness to extend their roles and share some responsibilities. In particular, staff in the private sector (e.g. Nursery Nurses) felt that they had less scope for development within their existing role than Nursery Officers (e.g. in Social Work Children/Family Centre settings). For example, a number of *key worker roles* were identified. These included being responsible for a child and for communication with the family; linking families to a range of services; carrying out assessments; outreach work;

coordination of service provision. A difference emerged between key worker roles that were limited to the early years settings and those roles that connected more to integrated working. Staff in private sector nurseries, play/out of school care settings and some HNC/VQ3 level staff (SCQF Level 7, EQF 5) in nursery schools/classes within education felt they were excluded from roles in integrated working.

All nursery staff pointed out the professional nature of their job. Many nursery staff felt that their roles were seen as inferior to nursery teachers. They argued that in education settings they were not given enough respon-sibility and contrasted this with the levels of autonomy experienced by nursery officers in Social Work Children/Family Centres. At the heart of their dissatisfaction was the feeling that they were not recognised as a pro-fession in their own right. A number of local authority and voluntary sector managers concurred with this perspective, arguing that the ability of nurs-ery workers to work as professionals with some level of autonomy should be more widely recognised.

Regular and Targeted Specialists

Many staff groups were keen to promote the specialist nature of their work. Nursery teachers were particularly keen that their specific skills in relation to curriculum development, assessment and working with children who required additional support be made available more often to children in early years settings. Some partner providers suggested that the provision of a universal teaching service should be free to all early years providers (whether public, private or voluntary) and that early years providers should be enabled to guar-antee parents and children a specific level of teacher input. Health visitors were also keen to maintain the specific nature of their work.

Some of the specialists who provided additional expertise or services were defined as 'Regular Specialists', that is they were attached to EECC centres (in education and social work) and in very regular contact with staff, children and families within these settings and on an outreach basis. This group included teachers, health visitors and a variety of outreach workers. Some children and families also experienced assessment by or support from 'Targeted Specialists'. This included, for example, social workers, educational psychologists, speech and language therapists and other health-related specialists. The way that staff were deployed and the competencies they utilised were influenced by the rhythm of their work; for example, whether they were involved in providing universal, targeted, daily, regular, scheduled or 'as and when' services depending on the context of the early years provision.

In short, Davis and Hughes (2005) found two groups of specialist early years staff:

- Staff in a range of Early Education and Childcare (EECC) settings who provided daily/regular support for learning, development and care

- Staff in health and social services who provided targeted, peripatetic, clinic based or intensive/short-term support for learning, development or care.

They found the first group of workers viewed themselves to be at the core of early years services. The staff in the second group viewed themselves as contributing to or having responsibilities in early years but within wider roles.

Role Extension

There was support for some workers having more generic knowledge and skills but in a context in which they could still access specialist/professional support and not lose their professional identity. For example, some health visitors and service managers could see the benefits of extending their roles, in some cases by being attached to an early years centre, in others by sharing skills and existing work roles with early education and childcare staff. Some teachers and education managers also saw value in extending their roles in relation to joint working in integrated services. Many staff highlighted the need to preserve particular lines of accountability, the need for protocols for sharing confidential information between staff in various services and the need for staff development for all staff in areas including assessment, report writing and confidentiality. However, despite this willingness to be adaptable in relation to integrated working, none of the specialist staff wanted their roles to be merged into a generic children's practitioner/ pedagogue role.

Most discussions concerning extended roles focused on the role of nursery nurses and nursery officers who form the majority of the workforce at practitioner level. There was considerable support across the workforce for the development of an extended role for nursery nurses and nursery officers in integrated early years services. Workers and managers in health, education and social work as well as nursery nurses themselves supported this. There was also considerable support for qualifications/opportunities that would enable nursery nurses and nursery officers to undertake management roles and/or have their existing management experience further accredited.

Training and Development

There was a great difference in qualifications held by staff in the public, private and voluntary sectors, with the least qualifications being held by staff in the private sector. There was a high level of interest among the workforce in gaining further qualifications. Of those qualified at Support Worker level, 70% wanted further qualifications. Of those qualified at practitioner level (e.g. HNC), 66% were keen to gain further advanced qualifications. Forty-four per cent wanted a SCQF Level 8/HND level award (e.g. further education college professional development award (PDA) or vocational management qualification such as VQ4) and 22% wanted degrees. (Please note since the study the required award for registration at manager level has moved from Level 8 to degree level, hence it is sensible to assume that the Level 8 group will now also be seeking degrees.)

Staff suggested they needed further training (CPD) on child development, promoting behaviour, group work, working with parents, inter-agency working, reducing risk, improving health and well-being, managing services and fostering inclusion. In the main, staff were very positive about the potential to expand their own roles and keen to take up training opportunities. It was specifically suggested that areas of development include the extension of child protection knowledge of early years practitioners/nursery nurses/teachers and the development of outreach work/more flexible work roles in private and education nurseries.

Many staff did not feel skilled in the areas of helping communities to develop, enhancing training and employment opportunities, developing cross-sector integrated professional practice and managing services to provide a more integrated response to children and families (Davis and Hughes, 2005).

Managers were keen for staff to be involved in joint training, processes of continuous review and professional development and for there to be clarity about what training was available and equity in the provision of training across services. Some local authority managers were able to give examples of good practice on workforce development (e.g. increased up-take of HNC, development of a degree for early years managers, funded training for childminders, joint training around child protection, etc.). However, perceived barriers to staff development and training included a lack of resources, time, opportunities, choice and support from senior colleagues.

In relation to training and continuing professional development, it was concluded that the workforce generally wanted to develop itself, to enhance current service provision and to develop in relation to the needs of integrated services. It was concluded that there was tremendous potential to link the emergence of integrated services to the development of joint training opportunities and a clearer career structure in early years. It was also argued that new initiatives should recognise and harness the aspirations of staff. Davis and Hughes (2005) argued that careful consideration should be given to a career structure which provided development, promotion and pay incentives to keep staff in the workforce, help them progress through qualification levels and (when qualified at degree level) enable them to undertake leadership and management roles. Greater clarity was required concerning the basic roles and responsibilities to be undertaken at each pay grade and what additional roles, responsibilities or tasks lead to upgrading.

Integrated and Co-located Teams, Centres and Services

In many cases, staff and mangers' ideas of joint working were limited because they were based on the premise that other services should join in with their existing practices (e.g. that staff should be seconded to their service) or that joint working meant collaboration between targeted and specialist professionals in their own field and not merged or systematic working across areas. Despite this perspective, there was a great deal of support amongst early years practitioners, nursery nurses (education), nursery officers (social work) and local authority area managers for the development of properly resourced early years integrated centres and the extension of Children and Family Centres. Some managers argued that proper planning of resources and roles would be key to any innovation. They suggested that innovation would not be easy and could not be developed overnight (not least because education managers felt that any change in the management structure of nursery provision would have to be managed in a sensitive manner).

It was argued that a new integrated service approach would have to break down traditional boundaries in education that resulted in services failing to meet families' needs during, for example, school vacations. Early years centres were thought to provide the potential to draw in services from outside education or social work, for example community/adult education, health and housing clinics. Neighbourhood working and joint team building were seen as key elements of the development of integrated working. Some managers promoted the idea that centre and neighbourhood managers could be appointed from across disciplines. It was suggested that this might require staff to have two lines of management. One line would relate to their co-located status, the other to their professional, specialist and statutory obligations. It was specifically suggested that specialist professionals might be more willing to accept line management from a professional not of their specialism if they also were able to access regular supervision/mentoring from a member of their profession.

Activity

Having a look at Chapter 2 again, can you see connections between the discussion in that chapter and this case study? Consider the different perspectives above and apply them to your workplace. For example, do you think that resources are more important than structures? To what extent does the case study above connect with the idea in Chapter 2 that integrated working is about building strong relationships and conceptual integration? At the time Davis and Hughes (2005) carried out their project there had been less research on integrated working. This might explain why there was a lack of discussion about conceptual differences and why professionals were concentrating on issues of identity, role and structure. Similarly, a number of publications had recently stressed the need for merger of early years into education services, the need for greater co-operation between public, private and voluntary services, and the benefits of a generic work role (e.g. pedagogue) (Cohen et al., 2004; Moss and Petrie, 2002; OECD, 2001). This context might explain the focus of Davis and Hughes's (2005) report. It would be worth considering how these debates have moved on and what contemporary ideas concerning roles in integrated working mean for your professional role. For example, some writers have indicated that as a result of integration and movement from health to Sure Start services some professionals have lost their registration status and felt strong professional isolation (Fox, 2005; Hannon et al., 2005). How would you feel about that? Has this happened to you? In Chapter 2 we saw that some writers argued that adopting an integrated team identity could be an extremely rewarding experience (Anning et al., 2006). Are you convinced?

Case Study Summary

To quickly summarise, Davis and Hughes (2005) found:

- workforce readiness for more integrated working

- workforce aspiration concerning qualifications and training

- workforce training gaps in community work, management, integrated working and promoting parental employment/careers

- workforce willingness for extension of the early years practitioner role and for early years practitioners to be recognised as a profession in their own right, given more autonomy, and provided with a career structure (including a degree-level management post)

- a need to clarify the role of core and specialist staff and to overcome professional snobbery/hierarchy.

Other studies suggest the keys to effective early years provision are a systematic/integrated approach; a fusing of care/education; universal access/public funding; training/qualifications; evaluation/monitoring; and the involvement of children/parents (OECD, 2001, 2006). In particular, a number of steps in the process have been recommended: the development of free/subsidised access to a high-quality universal service; a single workforce (e.g. the development of the early years teacher in New Zealand); a single regulatory framework; and the development of an integrative philosophy (e.g. pedagogy) that merges the concepts of education and care (Moss and Bennett, 2006).

The remainder of this section will discuss what an integrated early years and play sector might look like, the problems of linking early years and schooling and a potential model of integrated early care/education.

Discussion: Structural Integrating of Care/Education

The integration of care and education in early years is perceived to be a key aspect of quality provision (Moss and Bennett, 2006). Children are thought to do better in fully integrated settings that combine care and education (Clark and Waller, 2007).

Some writers have argued that greater integration requires the placing of early years within education ministries (e.g. as occurred in Sweden) (Cohen et al., 2004). It is argued that this has benefits because: the main focus of education is on the child; it leads to co-location of daycare, early years and schooling services; it enables a lifelong learning approach to be taken that allows greater synthesis across pre-school, school and beyond; it allows for the development of staff teams; it enables an integrated day at the level of pedagogy (a holistic approach to the child across out of school care/school); and it provides a better basis for developing universal provision (Cohen et al., 2004; Moss and Bennett, 2006). Research has suggested that the best quality provision occurs where the integration of care/education is combined with well-qualified staff, interactive relationships and a proportion of trained teachers (Pugh, 2010; Sylva, et al., 2004). Whilst these appear at first sight to be eminently sensible positions, it is important that we do not conflate issues of ministerial oversight, structural integration, conceptual integration, free/subsidised universal provision and staff development/qualifications. They are separate yet interlinked issues.

Attempts to structurally integrate play, health, childcare (mainly private sector) and early education (mainly public sector) occurred with regards to Sure Start initiatives and Early Excellence centres in England (Pugh, 2010). In particular, Early Excellence centres have combined adult education, parent support and integrated care/education (Pugh, 2010). Some initiatives in England claim that there have been real benefits from structural change,

(Continued)

(Continued)

for example where midwives and health visitors have been quickly integrated into Sure Start/Children's Centres and subsequent local children's trusts (Billingham and Barnes, 2009; Hawker, 2010).

In Brighton, England, Children's Centres were placed in 'poor' areas. The provision was transformed by enabling the centres to have a high proportion of nursery teachers, experienced managers and a full multidisciplinary team (including health visitors). The Children's Centres now attract families from a range of economic backgrounds and provide flexible full daycare from birth to four (Hawker, 2010). Co-location also worked well in Islington, England, where some Children's Centres have been located in primary schools, as well as private and voluntary sector early years providers. This has enabled families to access a range of provision, including reception, nursery, birth to three, stay & play, family support, health, and training/employment advice (Rudge, 2010).

Children's trusts and joint commissioning in local areas between the local authority and primary care trust resulted in partners developing binding commitments to joint action and a shared agenda (Hawker, 2010). The Children's Centres were based on a wholly integrated service model that required some staff to adopt new roles in relation to themselves and their clients (Hawker, 2010). A number of staff groups had to significantly change their roles, carry out retraining and provide on-site provision. It was argued that this change supported professionalism rather than undermining it (Hawker, 2010).

Activity

Chapter 2 highlighted the keys to integrated working as being structural, conceptual and relational. The integration of care, health and education in Brighton (that required professional re-alignment) came about from the centre and resulted in the reworking of locations and greater links between the private, voluntary and public sector. Can you identify such initiatives in your local areas? Can you use the definitions of integrated working from Chapter 2 to identify whether they involve cooperation, collaboration, co-ordination or merger? For example, in the case of Brighton the new service involved greater co-ordination, more central control and a shift to shared agendas (Hawker, 2010). However, it did not result in the merger of education/health systems.

The Problems of Structural Integration of Early Years, Health, Play and Schooling

The high priority attached to cross-agency work and joined-up services in the UK is not apparent in Sweden where families experience greater welfare provision provided by higher taxes (Cohen et al., 2004). Some writers argue that the emergence of discourses concerning integrated working may reflect the failure of government in the UK to properly address welfare issues and issues of poverty (Clarke and Newman, 1997; Riddell and Tett, 2001).

The shift to Children's Centres in Brighton encountered problems particularly in relation to difficulties balancing local autonomy with central control and the requirement for increased costs to be supported by Westminster funding (Hawker, 2010). Other writers have argued that there can be problems with leadership in early years integrated centres that is top-down at the strategic level and collaborative at team level (e.g. when decisions over staffing, finance and equipment are overturned) (Aubrey, 2010). There is no doubt that proper financing of early years services and provision of universal access is a key aspect of producing high-quality provision. This issue should not be conflated with discussions concerning schooling as a universal provision or discussions about who should manage and lead early years provision.

The Davis and Hughes (2005) study found that not all staff agreed that co-location had benefits. Some managers argued that shared planning would be easier to achieve than integrated centres and that this would have benefits for service delivery and resourcing. The issue of joint planning was often linked to a concern that service development should concentrate on improving outcomes for parents and children rather than promoting structural change. Some managers argued that increased resources were more important than changes to the location of services. Some frontline staff argued that large centres might restrict the ability of staff to find creative service solutions and that they themselves might be prevented from finding solutions because they were isolated from other specialists.

There is some suggestion from research in New Zealand that improvements in individual services relate more to increased training/qualification than to structural change. For example, by 2006 the 2002–2012 early years strategy had only accounted for a 1% increase in the number of children accessing Early Childhood Education services, the overall quality of services had not changed and there were still disproportionate levels of access for children from less well-off families (Mitchell and Hodgen, 2008). Increases in the quality of individual services were related to increased qualifications of the lead professional rather than a change in the overall system.

The adoption of an early years teacher-led model in New Zealand related to traditional conceptual resistance by the early years sector towards the ideas of schooling (Cohen et al., 2004). Some writers have argued that the separation of education and care in Scotland was traditionally related to the fact that daycare was viewed as a means to an end (e.g. allowing parents to work)

(Cohen et al., 2004). However, this underplays the history and nature of daycare and early years in Scotland (which has some similarities with New Zealand). For example, there has been a strong tradition in Scotland of separating out of school care, play and early years provision from schooling. This has occurred because of a wish to avoid schoolification (excessive emphasis on formal learning) and an aspiration to take a child-centred holistic approach. Some writers explain this philosophical gap in terms of the different traditions of care (nurses and nannies) and education (teaching) (Whalley, 1994). In England there has, over time, been a strong response in the daycare sector to, for example, the early introduction of children into primary education (Brown, 1994; Clark and Waller, 2007). Similarly, a 'readiness for school' type curriculum in early childhood settings is thought to be poorly suited to children and counter to integrated/holistic approaches (e.g. such as those enshrined in the idea of pedagogy) (David et al., 2010; OECD, 2006).

Indeed, a number of authors have cautioned that the merger of care and education in Sweden resulted in some schoolification of early years and day/ out of school care, that there was a tendency for those within compulsory schooling to treat other services as the junior partner, and that more research was needed into this area (Cohen et al., 2004; Moss and Bennett, 2006).

There would be great resistance in Scotland to any process that increased schoolification of early years. Davis and Hughes (2005) found that some early years practitioners in education nursery schools/classes indicated that hierarchical assumptions about the superiority of teachers created professional snobbery and led to discrimination (e.g. the calling of student teachers/teachers Mr/Mrs/Miss and early years practitioners by their first names; the exclusion of early years practitioners from meetings; and the hierarchical imposition of duties). In the most hierarchical of settings, teachers avoided care activities, some peripatetic teachers had little contact with children and early years practitioners carried out assessments (and other duties) that were supposed to be carried out by the teacher.

In England there has also been tension between Sure Start workers and health visitors concerning role clarification, use of scarce resources and an unwillingness to undertake more mundane tasks (Rowe, 2005). Other authors have indicated that there have been problems between health and integrated services, for example where health was not the lead agency they were found to be reluctant to share information (Billingham and Barnes, 2009). Some authors raise the issue of how difficult it is to get recognition for innovative integrated programmes from statutory services and that specific professionals in key positions find it difficult to accept new ways of working (Fox, 2005). Similarly, local politics and vested interest can result in social work and health services failing to fully support new initiatives (Smith and Davis, 2010). Staff in integrated teams have indicated that they have had real difficulties getting social workers, midwives, health visitors and Sure Start local peer workers to adopt a common language/ aims and to stop vying for position. In some cases, specific services (e.g. social work and educational psychology) have been found to have no defined case load, see very few children/families and make a very small amount of home visits (Aubrey, 2010). Some social workers and educational psychologists were found to only provide general support outside of statutory processes (e.g. those related to children at risk, in care or experiencing disability). Some leaders of social work and psychology argued that they were neither staffed nor resourced to provide pre-school indirect service delivery.

In contrast to the limited approach of some social work and educational psychology services, other professionals have clearly articulated what they add to integrated working. For example, speech and language therapists have worked to agreed targets, increased the number of children overcoming communication, language and literacy issues, provided advice to local staff, delivered training to staff/parents/professionals, carried out joint assessments, performed home visits and actually worked with children (Aubrey, 2010). They were able to clearly articulate what their knowledge base and aims were (Aubrey, 2010). They worked at a preventative level for the majority of children but provided specialist intervention for the small number of children who required it. They also carried out evaluations of their service, audits of children and collaborated with others to develop innovative approaches (Aubrey, 2010).

Similarly, in Scotland the emergence of the innovative integrated family work degree-led professional role was found to have had a positive impact on families (Smith and Davis, 2010). These professionals worked across different tiers of services providing a single agency frontline early intervention service; worked with children in schools/early years provision; carried out development work in people's homes; provided joint/targeted working at community level (e.g. group work in schools); imparted targeted/acute provision to families; and collaborated on multi-agency assessment/planning at local authority level (e.g. in area integrated forums) (Smith and Davis, 2010). Some family workers have come with degrees in social work, nursing or community education. Others have taken the BA degree in Childhood Practice.

The key distinction here is the relationship built with early years professionals, parents and children. A number of writers have highlighted the importance of working with children and families at the same time and have been critical of the tradition in social work daycare services of working with children in isolation (Dolan, 2006, 2008; Whalley, 1994). Parental involvement is central to the development of good early years settings (Desforges and Abouchaar, 2003; Pugh, 2010). The development of the early years strategy in New Zealand was criticised for ignoring the importance of family work and placing too much emphasis on early years care and education services (Shulruf, 2009). Ecological approaches are believed to require that early childhood services address issues in both childcare and family settings (Smith et al., 2000). In particular, a holistic approach to children and families has been related to the principles of Te Whāriki (the early childhood curriculum) that connected issues of well-being, belonging, relationships, communication, exploration, contribution, family, community, ethnicity, rights, diversity and culture (David et al., 2010; Smith et al., 2000).

There appears to be no appetite in Scotland for the structural merger of early years, play and schooling but there is an aspiration to work in a more integrated way with children and families. In the literature, there appear to be conflicting views concerning the benefits of integrating early years with other services and the role of different professionals within early years. This raises important questions concerning what different professionals do. Who manages integrated early years services? Who delivers daily services? Who provides regular specialist provision (including contact with children and families)? Who provides targeted provision? At the centre of these questions lies the aspiration that we maximise the use of resources and do not waste them on haphazard, ill-defined and non-evaluated input from expensive individuals.

Davis and Hughes (2005) found that most professionals felt ill-prepared for integrated working. In particular, there was a lack of knowledge/skills concerning management of integrated services. In New Zealand in 2003, 36% of early childhood education services had no integrated contact with other services (Mitchell and Hodgen, 2008). This figure remained unchanged in 2006. Insufficient time was highlighted as the key barrier to more integrated working (Mitchell and Hodgen, 2008). Many writers argue that training is a key aspect that aids the shift to more integrated approaches (Leathard, 2003a and b; Marks, 1994; Milne, 2005; Scott, 2006; Stone and Rixon, 2008).

Activity

What training have you and your colleagues received regarding integrated working? In a team meeting can you create a chart and note down where the training took place, the background of the people providing the training, who funded it, how long it occurred for (e.g. half day, day, short course, long course, initial professional training degree, etc.), and whether it was accredited/CPD? What does the chart tell you?

(Continued)

(Continued)

Aubrey (2010) argues that effective integrated working requires clear contracting, service level agreements, clear job specifications and proper evaluation. If you are a student can you discuss these issues with people you know that work in integrated services? What barriers have they encountered? If you are a practitioner or manager, is your role clear with regard to integrated working? Can you create a visual diagram of the people who work with children in your location? Are they regular, core staff, specialists or part of an integrated team? Do you know the professional backgrounds of the people you work with? Does this matter? What more could be done to create clear roles?

A Potential Model of Integrated Early Care/Education

Davis and Hughes (2005) captured staff fears concerning their structural location within integrated working. In particular, there were tensions concerning manger and practitioner roles. Some writers have privileged the role of teachers in the early years setting, putting them at the centre of models and assuming they are natural leaders/managers (see e.g. Nutbrown, 1994; Sylva et al., 2004). Davis and Hughes (2005) found that in education settings the assumption was that the manager would be a teacher. Such assumptions ignore less Anglo-centric work that emphasises the need for early years managers to have a degree and an understanding of community development (OECD, 2001, 2006). Indeed, the Davis and Hughes (2005) study found that teachers felt management duties drew them away from their core work (working with children) and that they had not received enough training on management issues in their original professional qualifications.

Similarly, in health it has been argued that the health visitor's role as the predominant universal service for children aged birth to three leaves them well placed to act in integrated centres as managers, co-ordinators or practitioners; for example, health visitors have taken responsibility for the management of home-visiting services and are believed to be able to better target/connect mothers to early intervention services (e.g. mental health) (Hawker, 2010).

However, some studies into integrated services have found health visitors to be as reticent as teachers, social workers and educational psychologists. For example, health visitors in England have voiced concerns about the movement away from family visiting, the shift to a needs based approach and debates concerning whether health visiting should be a universal or targeted service (Blackburn, 1994). They have raised issues regarding the need to provide advice/support to families on how to maximise the benefits they claim and the expectation they would carry out some form of social policing that might overlap with the child protection duties of social work (Blackburn, 1994). It was argued that sometimes this detracted from core health promotion work, for example supporting mothers, building family/community partnerships and campaigning/raising awareness/providing information on health issues (Blackburn, 1994).

The participants in Davis and Hughes's (2005) study suggest that the concept of 'teacher led' or 'health visitor led' services conflates notions of leadership and management and that it is possible for health visitors, teachers, etc. to lead on key aspects of provision and for the early years manager to lead the provision as a whole. In particular, Davis and Hughes found support for the retention of the non-managerial specialist titles and roles 'early years teacher' and 'health visitor'. They also found that these professionals aspired for their work to be more focused and defined in integrated early years settings.

Davis and Hughes (2005) found that not all settings were the same. For example, some nursery schools/classes overcame the boundary between care and education and each professional was respected for their contribution whatever their background. In particular, a number of education managers indicated that this shift was dependent on the separation of the manager and teacher role. They indicated that in a number of Scottish local authorities the early years practitioner had adopted the manager's role and the teacher now worked with them. This finding is similar to that of other writers who suggest that there are different types of management/supervision in early years (e.g. profession led, team manager, joint/shared management) and different types of leadership (e.g. coaching/mentoring/guiding, strategic, motivating, entrepreneurial) (Aubrey, 2010).

Some writers argue that heads/leaders of integrated Children's Centres need a wide range of knowledge of young children's learning based on practical experience but that high-quality provision also requires a multi-skilled workforce including teachers and professionals from health, social care and employment (Rudge, 2010). Quality integrated early years provision is believed to require workers from different agencies and professional backgrounds to be brought together to work towards a common aim and to extend their work beyond their conventional roles (Hannon et al., 2005). It is argued that integrated centres need to be run in a way that enables all staff (whatever their profession) to make an equal contribution (Billingham and Barnes, 2009; Hawker, 2010).

Within this context, early years management posts (e.g. Children's Centre managers) are characterised as involving the co-ordination of multiple tasks, staff teams and projects and are believed to require managers to have the ability to devolve power to project leaders (Aubrey, 2010). Davis and Hughes (2005) concluded that different models existed for early years centres, for example with specific professionals (teachers, social workers, adult education workers, careers staff, community workers, health visitors, psychologists and speech/language therapists) characterised as daily, regular or targeted specialists. It is important to note that movements towards integrated working in Scotland have involved a great deal of local variation. This chapter concludes that rather than proposing a specific best model, it is more important to ensure that professional roles within integrated early years settings are clear, cost-effective and what children/parents want. This conclusion suggests that whatever the balance of professionals (e.g. daily, regular and targeted) and interventions (e.g. frontline, compensatory, preventative and acute) clarity is key. It is possible to conclude that the processes of clarifying different professional roles requires specialist roles not to be conflated with centre management roles.

Since the Davis and Hughes (2005) study, the new Degree in Childhood Practice has been developed for early years, play and daycare centre lead practitioners/managers in Scotland (QAAS, 2007). Many writers have highlighted the need for such a degree in early years (Pugh, 2010). The standards for the degree set out the knowledge, skills and values expected of such staff. The standards were developed by a cross-sector technical expert group covering employers, further education, training providers, higher education, government, the Scottish Qualifications Authority, the Scottish Social Service Council and representatives from various umbrella organisations/associations. The Scottish Social Services Council has made this qualification a requirement for registration at manager level. However, this qualification has also become popular with assistant family workers who are seeking promotion to a degree-level family worker role and staff in the voluntary sector who are seeking a degree that accredits their work for children's organisations. The degree and registration requirements support other initiatives aimed at increasing the quality of early education and care services in Scotland (e.g. the development of a single qualifications framework, local childcare partnerships including public/voluntary/private sector providers, curriculum for excellence and an early years framework).

The standards emphasise the connection between theory, policy and practice and the importance of integrated, community based, participatory, anti-discriminatory and holistic approaches to children and families. They could be said to encompass the best traditions of pedagogical approaches that start with the whole child, mind, emotions, creativity, history and social identity (Cohen et al., 2004) and that, for example, see care and learning as inseparable, pedagogy as an integrative concept that transcends care, education and health, and children as active competent learners who create/co-construct knowledge (Cohen et al., 2004). Childhood practitioners like pedagogues are expected to have time for thought (local discussion and reflection), work in environments that provoke critical thinking (reading and discussion), be able to carry out analysis for change (considering research and theory) and develop strategies for change (at a political level) (Cohen et al., 2004). In the most part in Scotland, it is this professional manager (as is the case in Children's Centres in England) who needs to ensure conceptual integration between a range of professionals. This process is made easier by recent recognition that strengths based approaches should be at the centre of integrative practice. In particular it tasks leaders/managers to create spaces of dialogue and networks of support for conceptual integration (Moss and Petrie, 2002). Within local settings (e.g. childcare partnerships that connect voluntary, private and public providers), this may include collaboration not just with the list of daily, regular and target professionals outlined above, but with those that take leadership roles and/or provide preventative/therapeutic support networks in local communities (e.g. playgroups: Brown [1994] or childminding association advisors: Warner [1994]).

Conceptual Integration in Scotland – the Childhood Practice Degree

Some have called for a new children's services professional role, covering, youth, community, social care, mental health and careers work (Cohen et al., 2004; Kendall and Harker, 2002). Also note that some staff in Sure Start provision in England have shown enthusiasm for a new hybrid profession (Aubrey, 2010).

However, it is important that early years developments do not privilege any one country's approach (David et al., 2010). Whilst this chapter has some sympathy for the position that a hybrid professional role would aid conceptual integration, Davis and Hughes (2005) demonstrate that it is not a development that can be quickly achieved in Scotland without conflict. It should also be noted, somewhat ironically, that whilst many schools in Sweden have substantial input from nurses and social workers, there is no suggestion that they might develop a new profession covering education, childcare, health and social work (Cohen et al., 2004).

At present, the Childhood Practice qualification has provided the focus for the development of a hybrid professional role in early years, Social Work Children/ Family Centres, play and out-of-school provision in Scotland. It is being viewed as the qualification of choice by some professionals in family work, children's voluntary organisations and residential childcare. Some early years managers, originally trained in social work or teaching, are now taking Childhood Practice courses as part of CPD. The Childhood Practice qualification has provided the basis for staff with contemporary ideas to challenge outdated and deficit approaches to children/families (such as have traditionally been found in social work daycare settings (see Whalley, 1994) or approaches that place too much emphasis on future attainment (e.g. Sylva et al., 2004)). At worst, aspects of the Childhood Practice degree should become core to initial training for all professionals that work with children in Scotland. Initial training should involve multi-disciplinary classes (or joint academic years) and existing professionals should be required to carry out multi-disciplinary continuing professional development on key aspects of Childhood Practice (e.g. a strengths based approach, pedagogy, a range of childhood theories, anti-discrimination, social justice and integrated working). It should also be recognised that most professionals who work with children already have aspects of pedagogy in their practice. Davis and Hughes (2005) found a number of common roles and concepts. It should be possible to utilise initial training and CPD to enable professionals to make conceptual connections. Once their similarities become apparent, it may be that resistance to a hybrid profession reduces.

Conclusion

This chapter has highlighted the difference between structural and conceptual integration in early years. It has concluded that the process of enabling conceptual integration through the development of a hybrid workforce will be difficult. It has also indicated that there is conceptual resistance in Scotland to the structural merger of schooling, play, day-care, out of school and early years. It has argued that structural change is possible in local settings where the role of managers and professionals does not become conflated; change is not top-down; one professional grouping does not dominate others; roles are clear; targets are agreed; professionals actually work with children/families; and there is a balance of daily, regular and targeted work. It has been concluded that quality early years provision requires a well qualified and balanced workforce. The degree-level Childhood Practitioner (e.g. early years centre manager) has been characterised as a person who can strive to enable conceptual integration between the different professionals. The Childhood Practice qualification has been represented as providing a possible basis for multi-disciplinary training that enables conceptual integration around the idea of a strengths based approach, pedagogy, a range of childhood theories, anti-discrimination, social justice and integrated working. These issues are discussed further in the next chapter.

Integrated Children's Services and Ethnicity

Chapter Overview

This chapter includes extracts from the executive summary report of a project carried out with Andy Hancock of the University of Edinburgh. These are included with the kind permission of Andy Hancock. This chapter considers the findings from a study in Scotland into early years services for black and minority ethnic families (Davis and Hancock, 2007). It considers how integrated children and family services can be located within communities, enable employment opportunities, and take into account users' experiences of services. It asks readers to compare the case study to approaches from outside the UK (e.g. Canada) and to their own practice/organisational systems. It encourages practitioners to move beyond stereotypes of 'minority ethnic' children and families and to consider: how they can more effectively work in this field; whether their practice enables families to self-empower; and how they can build partnerships with children and families from diverse communities. This chapter concludes that barriers still exist for some black and minority ethnic families in accessing children and family services; there is a distinction between writing that gives helpful advice on how to deal with such barriers and writing that connects issues of anti-discrimination, equity and social justice to the ability of children's services to develop collaborative, capacity-building, integrative and systematic approaches to working with communities; and that such approaches put the participation of children, parents and community members at the centre of service development.

Black and Ethnic Minority Families' Use of Early Years Services

This project was carried out between 2006 and 2007. It involved a questionnaire distributed to service providers and qualitative group discussions with parents, staff and managers.

The study had a number of aims:

- To review the legislative and policy framework for provision of services for black and minority ethnic families

- To write a literature review of the research in relation to black and minority ethnic families' use of early years services

- To audit and identify gaps in the existing service design

- To assess the relevance, scope and scale of existing children and family services in relation to needs of black and minority ethnic families and identification of the gaps

- To review access to services for black and minority ethnic families

- To consider recommendations for a strategy on developing the service to better meet needs and improve access (Davis and Hancock, 2007).

Profile of Service Use and Staffing

In Scotland, at policy level, the term early years services is increasingly being used to provide an encompassing term for care and education services. In the literature, Early Education and Childcare (EECC) and Early Childhood Education and Care (ECEC) are frequently used. In the workplace and community, terms like nursery education and daycare, nursery school/class, day nursery and children's centre are more common. The use of these various terms represents the variety of perspectives and diversity of understanding about purposes and functions of services (Davis and Hancock, 2007). Information on school pupils' ethnicity, home language and English as an Additional Language (EAL) categories were available from the Council's Information and Research section as part of statutory requirements for the annual school census and ScotXed (the educational analytical service of the Scottish government). However, comprehensive quantitative data of this type was particularly difficult to access for pre-school provision. Without this valuable data any patterns of inequality or shortcomings in provision cannot be easily identified (Davis and Hancock, 2007).

The results of the questionnaire indicated that there was a sizeable black and minority ethnic community living within the local area who sent their children to a range of childcare and education service providers. The main ethnic groups were Pakistani, Polish, Chinese and Indian. A number of staff discussed the different challenges faced with the arrival of families from the new EU accession states, especially Poland. The questionnaire showed a significant number (second largest category) of children of mixed heritage. The results of the questionnaire confirmed that most of the service users remain overwhelmingly 'white' with children with ethnic, cultural and linguistic variation being scattered thinly across services (with the vast majority of providers having few children from black and minority ethnic heritages) (Davis and Hancock, 2007).

Davis and Hancock (2007) found the profile of the early years/childcare worker was predominantly female (94.6%) and white (94%) and covered a range of age groups (between 16 and 55). Over two-thirds of the providers employed no black and minority ethnic staff. Staff came from a variety of black and minority ethnic backgrounds and from a range of minority ethnic groups. The main ethnic groups by nationality were Polish, Indian, Pakistani and Black African. A small number of childcare providers (8%) employed teaching and early years staff to specifically work with black and minority ethnic children. These settings had the largest concentrations of children from black and minority ethnic backgrounds.

Staff expressed a need for more recruitment of black and minority ethnic staff in the sector and raised concerns about the status of black and minority ethnic staff; the recognition of their qualifications, e.g. if gained abroad; and their career choices and opportunities for promotion. Increasing the number of minority ethnic staff was seen by black and minority ethnic parents to provide positive role models for their children and their interpreting skills were believed to support effective communication.

Davis and Hancock (2007) concluded that service providers should be encouraged to routinely use professional and trained interpreters. There was a clear need to increase opportunities for responsive interpreting (telephone interpreting), particularly to enable conflict resolution. Systems for accessing interpreters of different spoken language varieties (e.g. Arabic) needed to be reviewed. It was also concluded that translated advice and documentation made available to black and minority ethnic parents needed to be reviewed to make sure it was appropriate, accessible and available in alternative formats (e.g. generic nursery booklet, information on nature of learning within the early years curriculum).

Though parents did not discuss EAL (English as an additional language) support, staff emphasised the challenge of providing additional language support for children new to English, especially recent arrivals from the new European Union accession states. Staff wanted more EAL support. Parents felt that nurseries provided an ideal environment for their children to acquire 'English' through interaction and developing new friendships. However, they also expressed a desire to retain their home language (which raised issues concerning staff abilities to support the children's bi-lingualism). Parents considered communication to be generally good albeit not enough. The parents tended to be happy with organised, formal meetings but they reported that they would like more time to talk to staff about day-to-day matters. Parents were generally sympathetic to staff whom they felt were under pressure and therefore unavailable to discuss individual needs (Davis and Hancock, 2007).

Activity

Consider how you define ethnicity. In the section above, Davis and Hancock (2007) identify different groups of parents and staff who may require specific services. These included families who had recently come from a range of continents (including Europe) with different languages, religions and cultures but it also included children and families who were born in the UK. Should where a person is born affect the services they experience? How do we ensure that there is equity in the way different children and families experience our services?

Dialogue Between Families and Services

In the main the most positive findings came from local authority and voluntary sector settings who had a great deal of experience of working with black and minority ethnic children and families. The nature of a developing dialogue and partnerships between the home and the settings was given a great deal of attention by both staff and parents. Provision varied between settings, for example some parents felt staff were very conscientious, always providing interpreters (in some cases over and above what was required). Others spoke of never being offered an interpreter (Davis and Hancock, 2007).

Both parents and staff felt there was a need for more immediate and accessible interpreters for daily communication (e.g. occasions where a child was involved in a fight or was ill). The parents reported several examples of confusion, misunderstanding and upset, apparently resulting from cultural differences, misinterpretation or linguistic difficulties. These issues were wide-ranging, including matters such as diet/eating patterns, hygiene and safety, health matters, feedback on children's welfare, awareness of rights and procedures related to the assessment and identification of additional support needs beyond EAL, etc. (Davis and Hancock, 2007).

Although communication difficulties were considered a priority issue by staff and parents, Davis and Hancock (2007) found the use of interpreting services was patchy. Information available from the Interpretation and Translation Service (ITS) suggested a limited uptake for their services from early years providers. Interpreting was not always available for the spoken language required (e.g. Kurdish, Arabic). Some staff and parents expressed concern about confidentiality issues that arose in small linguistic communities where the interpreter was a member of the same community. Concerns were also raised about inappropriate involvement of children, relatives, staff or parents as interpreters. This seemed to be accepted as common practice by both agencies and parents with little concern for accompanying issues.

Parents in the main expressed overall satisfaction with their children's care. However, some parents, who were not offered the contact or information they desired, appeared to feel unsupported and disillusioned. Asked about the content of their children's day and activities, most parents commented on practical rather than pedagogic aspects. On occasions, there was a mismatch between parents' expectations of their children's learning experiences at nursery/early stages of primary school and those of the staff. For example, a number of parents were dissatisfied with the lack of homework and considered the academic standard in Scotland too low (Davis and Hancock, 2007).

Davis and Hancock (2007) found that a large percentage of providers never or very rarely invited black and minority ethnic community members to the premises on a regular basis to participate in activities (cultural or otherwise). Staff interviews suggested there was a desire to bring in black and minority ethnic parents to participate but there were issues of time as it was felt supervision and liaison with 'hesitant' parents would generate more work. When black and minority ethnic parents were asked about their involvement in their child's nursery, there were mixed responses. Where parents have been invited to participate and contribute to sessions, they expressed satisfaction and tended to be positive about the setting. Most parents, however, had no experience of participation, although virtually all indicated they would welcome it. One parent reported volunteering to help with a session, as she was aware of other parents having done so, only to be turned down. She ascribed this unequivocally to her ethnicity (Davis and Hancock, 2007).

Parents discussed a number of issues related to access to childcare which did not specifically relate to ethnicity; for example, there were many complaints about availability of nursery places, and calls for more funding for nursery places to be available to pre-3 children and for greater geographic accessibility. Problems included nursery hours being too short to allow parents to work, logistics of transport/travel and private nurseries being too costly (Davis and Hancock, 2007).

Activity

As a professional do you know what to do when interpreters are required? Have you had training on how to make this judgement in partnership with service users? Do you have protocols? Do the protocols say anything about the sensitivity of interpreting? How do you ensure that a service user is happy with the person identified as an interpreter? If you do not have a protocol could you raise this in a team meeting? If you are a student could you contact your local authority and ask them for a copy of their guidelines or protocols? Could you bring this to your class and discuss it with other students? In most cases provision is available. However, professionals do not always know how to access it.

Inclusive Early Years Service Provision

Davis and Hancock (2007) found that a large percentage of service providers had made explicit efforts to value and recognise diversity by providing linguistically and culturally diverse materials and resources. In addition, there was a good understanding of the faiths and traditions of minority ethnic families and celebrations of these regularly occurred within the settings. Most parents were happy with the resources/activities and approved of celebrations of multiculturalism.

Racism was perceived by parents as widespread across society, ranging from hostility and aggression to ignorance and condescension, but the majority of nurseries were not considered to involve racism. The most ethnically and culturally diverse early years settings were perceived by parents as being more equitable places and as demonstrating greater awareness of racism. Some parents were keen to move their children out of predominantly white settings to such early years settings because they were perceived to provide higher quality care. Parents felt racist bullying was generally not a problem amongst children until upper primary age (Davis and Hancock, 2007).

Some responses to the staff questionnaire indicated that an extremely small minority of staff did not welcome families with linguistic difference. These staff expressed a desire for families to assimilate into the dominant language and culture as quickly as possible (in some cases it was stated they should learn English before coming to Scotland) and showed little understanding of contemporary approaches to supporting language development. These staff usually based their cultural and linguistic assumptions on their previous experience of one child/family, had low-level qualifications and had received little training on equity issues (Davis and Hancock, 2007).

Some staff in voluntary, private and local authority providers who did not have diverse catchment areas showed little inclination to promote equity issues. They assumed that the promotion of race equality issues was only necessary in settings where children came from diverse backgrounds. These perceptions meant that guidance on promoting equity was overlooked as were opportunities to unpack the connectedness of equity issues such as immigration, poverty, disablism, sexism, homophobia, racism and social exclusion (Davis and Hancock, 2007). These staff assumed they worked in settings that lacked diverse families when the likelihood is that they did not. In so doing they overlooked the fact that early years staff need to offer all children support in developing positive attitudes towards all people and it is a great mistake to assume that equity issues are only relevant to largely multi-ethnic children/settings (Siraj-Blatchford, 2010).

In the most diverse settings, staff suggested that their service encouraged participation, integration and interaction between children of different ethnic groups. In other settings race equality was spoken of in terms of providing a multicultural curriculum and/or in limited terms such as, 'we treat them all the same'. Unlike staff, parents perceived race equality in broader terms that included the need to recognise individual identities, the right to effective communication with regard to their child's well-being/welfare, the need to overcome a lack of involvement in their child's nursery, and the existence of structural/institutional barriers when complaints were made about staff.

Davis and Hancock (2007) found that issues of racism in their study were not always overt. This is similar to other writing that suggests that underlying inequalities might remain hidden in early years settings and that disadvantage may be both intentional and unintentional (Siraj-Blatchford, 2010). This writing encourages us not to assume that all members of 'structurally oppressed groups' experience the same types of oppression because identity is multifaceted (Siraj-Blatchford, 2010). It also requires us to understand the different types of racism and that those that work with children may unintentionally undermine their self-esteem due to a connection of issues including gender, religion, socio-economic status, language or ethnicity (Figueroa, 1993; Siraj-Blatchford, 2010). For example, *cultural racism* involves a link between group identity, group world view and group behaviour (Figueroa, 1993).

Activity

Can you consider instances of cultural racism in the case above? If a group of parents are co-organising an event at a nursery but do not invite black and minority ethnic parents, that would be cultural racism. Social relations between groups are defined by their different cultural constructs. This can involve one group maintaining power over another group as a result of taken-for-granted forms of social interaction – if a nursery is serious about issues of equity then the manager needs to consider how power relations operate in his/her setting. Cultural racism can become *structural racism* if these power relations are integrated into the way a nursery is organised. Structural racism refers to the differential distribution on racist grounds of resources, rewards, roles, status and power (Figueroa, 1993). For example, concerns were raised in the above case that staff from black and minority ethnic backgrounds may be prevented from gaining promotion. Organisations have a duty to ensure that there is equity in promotion opportunities.

Individual racism is associated with individuals who hold stereotypical views and *interpersonal racism* involves discrimination, harassment and the articulation during social interaction of racist terms (Figueroa, 1993). In the case above there were very few instances of interpersonal racism; however, if those members of staff (in private sector settings) who felt people should 'learn English' before they come here had articulated this (individually racist) position to a service user and not just written it on our questionnaire then this would be a clear case of interpersonal racism.

Institutional racism manifests itself in the institutions of a society such as schools and functions to disadvantage certain groups by failing to take account of the needs of those groups (Figueroa, 1993). An example of institutional racism would be the operation of a culturally exclusive curriculum. This is an important issue because writers in the previous chapter assumed that pedagogical approaches always benefited children but some writers have suggested that the traditional child-centred and westernised play ethos approach of pedagogy may not work for children who have culturally different starting points to those providing the services (Brooker, 2002, 2005; Clark and Waller, 2007; Smith et al., 2000). We should never assume that one country's approach (e.g. that of Sweden) works in another (David et al., 2010). New Zealand is a much more culturally diverse country than Sweden and in the last chapter we looked at their Te Whāriki early childhood curriculum. Can you search the internet for examples of how the curriculum in New Zealand aims to avoid institutional racism?

Training, Awareness and Partnership

The Davis and Hancock (2007) study indicated that the EAL (English as an additional language) team provided training in specific establishments throughout the year. A multilingual video/DVD training pack had been produced by the local EAL service. Staff expressed a need for further training (CPD) on inclusion policies and practice (e.g. working alongside EAL staff and interpreters). In particular, more effort could have been made to connect local authority initiatives to the needs of local voluntary and private sector providers. There was a clear need for an expansion of anti-racist and anti-discriminatory training across settings (especially awareness raising amongst providers in predominantly 'white' areas). The local authority was committed to monitor, evaluate and update the Equalities Induction Pack (EIP) for all local authority staff but questions were raised regarding non-local authority providers. There was a need to develop and review strategies for supporting the promotion of anti-discriminatory practices in voluntary and private providers, in particular in relation to local workforce development funding. Examples of good practice, such as approaches to involving black and minority ethnic parents in settings, dual language book borrowing, links with community groups, translating websites, deployment of dedicated bilingual staff, etc., needed to be disseminated and developed across services through the creation of collaborative working and networking opportunities. There was a need to build upon EAL service capacity-building activities with early years providers to develop the workforce's ability to support children for whom English is an additional language. There was a need to increase resources within early years settings that reflected cultural and linguistic diversity (e.g. persona dolls) and to ensure that existing resources were used more effectively. Service providers were advised to review policies and practices on developing partnerships with black and minority ethnic parents and look at how they involved black and minority ethnic parents, on their own terms, in ways that they wanted and could manage. Davis and Hancock (2007) concluded that effective examples of involving black and minority ethnic parents needed to be analysed, evaluated, disseminated and taken forward in creative ways to fit local contexts. There was also a need for more effective communication and liaison between service providers and black and minority ethnic parents, more opportunities for open dialogue, and greater discussion concerning the nature of early years learning/pedagogical approaches. They also concluded that there was a need to additionally research the extent to which black and minority ethnic children were consulted on policies and provision that affected them and how their views then impacted on service development.

Summary of Project Findings

- Although there was evidence of greater childcare use across all black and minority ethnic groups following expansion of childcare services, barriers still existed for some black and minority ethnic families in accessing childcare.

- The profile of the early years worker was predominantly white and female. Only a small number of childcare providers employed staff specifically to work with black and minority ethnic children.

- Parents considered services to be responsive to developing channels of communication for formal occasions but both black and minority ethnic parents and staff felt there was a need for more immediate and accessible interpreters for daily communication.

- Parents who had been invited to participate and contribute to sessions expressed satisfaction and tended to be positive about the setting. However, a number of parents had no experience of participation in services.

- A large number of service providers had made overt efforts to value and recognise diversity by providing linguistically and culturally diverse materials and resources. In addition, there was a good understanding of the faiths and traditions of black and minority ethnic parents and celebrations of these regularly occurred within the settings.

- Racism was perceived by black and minority ethnic parents as widespread across society but not generally considered to be a problem amongst very young children. However, some black and minority ethnic parents were not happy with their provision and were keen to move their children to more diverse settings.

- There was a need to review the reliability and consistency of the information-gathering systems on up-take of services by the black and minority ethnic community, patterns of inequality in early years provision and instances of racism.

- There was a need to increase the recruitment and retention levels of black and minority ethnic staff.

- There was a clear need for an expansion of anti-racist and anti-discriminatory training across settings (especially awareness raising amongst providers in predominantly 'white' areas).

- It was believed that service providers should review policies and practices on developing partnerships with black and minority ethnic parents and look at how they involved black and minority ethnic parents.

- High-quality examples of participation with black and minority ethnic parents needed to be analysed, evaluated and disseminated (Davis and Hancock, 2007).

Discussion: Strengths Based v. Reactive Community Services

In Canada a number of initiatives have discussed the importance of developing community based integrated services with First Nation aboriginal people (Ball and Sones, 2004; Moore et al., 2005). They have argued that we need to build holistic provision that connects with local cultures, values and practices (Ball and Sones, 2004). At the centre of this discussion is the suggestion that non-Inuit professionals need to understand the socio-cultural history of the people they work with (for example, in less than 50 years the Inuit shifted from a subsistence, seasonal relocation, family centred way of living to a permanent housing position where families were fractured, many children were removed and taken very far away and adults were forced into the wage economy) (Dickson, 2004; Moore et al., 2005). This need, to understand the context of the lives of the people we work with, applies equally in Canada as it does to the social history of communities in the UK (e.g. ex-mining areas experienced tremendous upheaval in the UK in the 1980s). It is argued that because of such upheaval we need to concentrate on how to develop employment opportunities in the areas people come from – we need local facilities that enable access to a multi-disciplinary group of people and capacity development by local integrated teams (Ball and Sones, 2004; Moore et al., 2005).

Some authors have sought to define capacity building as those processes that address issues in the *local environment* (e.g. poverty, crime, poor housing); attempt to strengthen *local organisations* (e.g. through staff training, funding or policies); support *community social organisation* (e.g. informal support, social/group or bridging networks); and foster *community connectedness* (e.g. connect leaders/services/groups to local systems) (Chaskin, 2006).

Such approaches in Canada attempted to cross the boundaries between service provider and user to define local integrated services as something beyond the situation where service providers are outsiders and service users are powerless locals (Ball and Sones, 2004; Moore et al., 2005). These approaches questioned the notion that early years services should only be defined by their ability to make children meet academic 'school ready' criteria, achieve westernised notions of 'skills development' and behave in 'age appropriate' ways (see, for examples of such uniform tests of early years effectiveness, the research tools used by Sylva et al. [2004]).

(Continued)

(Continued)

It is argued that a shift in service development can be achieved if the different actors involved are willing to learn from each other and accept that children, young people, parents, professionals, relatives and various community members possess their own kinds of expertise which they can bring to processes of development (Davis, 2000; Moore et al., 2005). For example, amongst the Inuit, local Elders were perceived to have particular abilities that aided this process (being warm, respectful, genuine, supportive, trusting, practical, etc.) (Moore et al., 2005). Multi-cultural competence was seen as a key part of collaborative service development. The ability to speak about your feelings, respond to cultural variations concerning face-to-face contact/body language/non-verbal queues and understand cultural nuances (e.g. about the appropriateness of asking direct questions), were all identified as key aspects of relationship building in integrated service development (Moore et al., 2005). Some writers in the UK argue that staff in early years settings need to find a shared language with which to work with both minority ethnic and dual heritage children and we need to build awareness through policy and practice (Siraj-Blatchford, 2010). Similarly, such cultural competence approaches have been utilised in processes of family support in Asian and South Pacific communities (Cheung and Leung, 2006).

Ball and Sones (2004) highlighted how such culturally sensitive approaches enabled the development of a self-governance community health project that boosted local employment by developing work roles for community members (e.g. planning and delivering local services) and enabled local people to be central to the process of delivering services. It is argued that such developments require to be located in places where the community usually meets, underpinned by processes of mentoring, managed by visionary leaders and linked to accredited training (Ball and Sones, 2004). They are also perceived to benefit from being focused on family centred approaches that avoid imposing Eurocentric notions of assessment and should involve families from the start of the development, promote local choice/decision-making, and strengthen family/community self-help (Ball and Sones, 2004; Moore et al., 2005). Some writers differentiate between the way that professionals conceptually frame community based family support, suggesting that it can be seen as a context (for planning), a target (of intervention) or a unit (of identity/action) (Chaskin, 2006). They also outline different definitions of 'community based' (e.g. located in a community, involving relationship building and outreach, or as a way of connecting families to broader services/support systems) (Chaskin, 2006).

Davis and Hancock (2007) found that the settings that parents had most confidence in carried out all of the above functions. These early years centres had very strengths based and integrated approaches to service development for black and minority ethnic children and families. However,

(Continued)

(Continued)

these centres were in the minority. In the UK, there is a tendency for early years approaches to race and ethnicity to focus on 'educating' parents and children about racism and how to deal with racist incidents (e.g. Rixon, 2008a; Siraj-Blatchford, 2010). These approaches give very useful advice; for example, to ensure you make parents aware of your policies, develop topic work around the theme of difference, work restoratively with both the children who make offensive remarks and those who experience the remarks (Siraj-Blatchford, 2010). However, the Canadian examples suggest that we should avoid creating a false division between parents within a local setting and that by adopting culturally sensitive and strengths based approaches from the start, all parents and children should be made to feel central to developments within early years provision.

Davis and Hancock (2007) found that many parents aspired to be involved more in their nurseries. Such approaches have been developed in the UK where underlying values have been put at the centre of discussions. In these cases it has not been assumed that different people view collaborative practices as meaning the same thing. The local community has been viewed as heterogeneous and individual relationships have been connected to concepts of community responsibility (Broadhead et al., 2008; Glenny and Roaf, 2008). Such approaches attempt to intervene as early as possible in children's lives, to broaden out those who experience services and to avoid approaches that involve service rationing (Aldgate and Tunstill, 1995; Glenny and Roaf, 2008; McGhee and Waterhouse, 2002; Tisdall, 1997; Walker, 2008).

Sheffield's Children Centre is identified as a practical example of such provision (Broadhead et al., 2008). The centre has attempted to reconcile different, often conflicting views concerning cultural diversity in the local community, developed training/employment opportunities for local parents as providers of services, inspired cross mentoring between young and old community members, developed joint media projects with the local media school, and engineered practical community projects that cross national boundaries (Broadhead et al., 2008). Within such community based approaches, parents are found to define high-quality children's services workers (in keeping with the Canadian example) as people who are caring, warm and good listeners (Glenny and Roaf, 2008). In Chapter 2 we saw that many writers in the UK suggested that such integrated services require strong relationships to be built with both parents and children (Glenny and Roaf, 2008). The involvement of service users such as children and families in integrated service development was promoted by a number of authors (Foley, 2008; Leathard, 2003b). However, these writers also indicate that there can be problems with such approaches, for example some parents have problems working with more confident parents. These processes can also be injurious if parents are assumed to have

(Continued)

(Continued)

cultural capacity and therefore they need to be underpinned by long-term processes of community capacity building (Jones and Leverett, 2008). In Ireland, Dolan (2008) encourages communities to recognise the resources that immigrants bring with them and to utilise their values, skills and knowledge within processes of community development. This approach moves away from viewing immigrants in a deficit way as a drain on scarce resources and encourages us to recognise that all community members, whatever their difference, have something to offer to strengths based children and family services.

Conclusion

This chapter has discussed the changing nature of early years services, it has highlighted the strengths and weaknesses of early years services for black and minority ethnic families in a Scottish local authority area. Davis and Hancock (2007) concluded that barriers still existed for some black and minority ethnic families in accessing childcare; parents considered services to be responsive but there was a need for more immediate and accessible interpreters; parental involvement/participation in services could be increased; and that greater sharing of resources (e.g. knowledge) could occur between those identified as high quality service providers and those that had difficulties, including children from linguistically and culturally diverse families. The activities in this chapter have encouraged you to consider the diverse nature of racism and this chapter has also drawn connections to writing in Canada, Ireland and the UK that promotes a community and strengths based approach to service provisions. A distinction has been drawn between writing that gives helpful advice on how to deal with issues of racism (e.g. how to raise awareness amongst staff/parents/children) and writing that connects issues of anti-discrimination, equity and social justice to the ability of children's services to develop collaborative, capacity building, integrative and systematic approaches to working with communities. These approaches were found to integrate community members into services through volunteering, training and employment. In particular they adopted models of community governance. In later chapters we will discuss further the conceptual shift that is required by such approaches but it is safe to say that whatever their conceptual position, such approaches put the participation of children, parents and community members at the centre of service development.

5

Strategic Planning of Integrated Child and Adolescent Mental Health Services

This chapter includes information from a summary report (Davis, 2008) carried out for Durham and Darlington Child and Adolescent Mental Health Services. It is included with the kind permission of Mark Cain and Lorrae Rose of County Durham Primary Care Trust.

Chapter Overview

This chapter will enable practitioners to consider the key issues that young people believe underpin integrated child and adolescent mental health services. It discusses the development of a local mental health strategy, issues of prevalence, different professional approaches to assessment, participatory approaches and conceptual integration. It draws from a range of sources to consider the development of a participatory integrated child and adolescent mental health service in a local authority in England. It concludes that when integrated services do not confront conceptual differences and professional vested interests, parents, teachers, counsellors, psychologists and medical professionals can fall into the trap of labelling children and young people rather than making their wishes central to service development. It provides practitioners with ideas for developing partnerships/joint service strategies and makes suggestions concerning the development of a professional approach to conceptual integration.

In 1997 a strategy was agreed for the development of a local Child and Adolescent Mental Health Service in an area of England. The strategy raised issues concerning:

- the strengths and weaknesses of service provision

- assessed service needs

- present and future initiatives

- service characteristics and principles

- short/long-term objectives and outcomes

- detailed information to support the strategy.

The strategy aimed to:

- enable stakeholders to work together to plan, commission and provide services

- work towards joint commissioning and integrated service provision

- produce a strategy that was relevant to stakeholders

- develop an agreed tiered approach to service provision

- address gaps in service provision and liaison between tiers

- change the nature of service provision (e.g. make it more accessible, equitable, preventative, supportive, inclusive, participatory and collaborative)

- appoint specific staff, strengthen teams, develop training (including joint training) and improve accommodation

- create comprehensive information systems and systems of evaluation, monitoring and quality assurance.

Specific emphasis was placed on services that took account of young people who experience learning disabilities, physical disabilities and/or were offending. The strategy also connected with the development of National Service Framework standards which highlighted the need for young people to be consulted about the development of services, services/agencies to work in partnership, services to respond to the needs of a diverse population and to improve emergency arrangements.

Child and Adolescent Mental Health Services' Integrated Strategy Evaluation

In 2006, whilst working at the University of Edinburgh, I was commissioned to:

- investigate the extent to which the strategy had met its aims

- carry out a literature review of existing reports to investigate the evidence base for the future strategy and make recommendations

- carry out an in-depth evaluation of various previous reports and participatory approaches that had collected young people's views

- produce a short draft report of the findings

- facilitate a process of dialogue and develop key questions from the reports to put to stakeholders to inform them of the new draft strategy

- attend key stakeholder events and carry out follow-up meetings with staff from various service tiers

- carry out discussions with children, young people, parents and/or carers. (Davis, 2006)

The literature review of previous evaluations and reports included:

- local psychologists' reports on the prevalence of child and adolescent mental health

- a local university assessment of needs

- a local health service report on prevalence and treatment

- the strategic partnership agenda

- reports from a local children's rights service

- primary care model documents

- primary mental health workers' reviews

- a self-assessment matrix

- a Developing the Workforce report.

The literature review was compared to presentations delivered by a range of presenters at stakeholder events, including topics such as:

- infant and child well-being

- looked after children

- multi-agency working

- specialist CAMHS

- strategic partnerships

- Webster-Stratton (parenting programme).

As part of the project, I met with young people involved in work with a local children's rights organisation who put forward a variety of views concerning the old and new strategies.

Summary of Key Findings

The project had a number of key findings regarding:

- achievements of the 1997 strategy

- estimating prevalence; defining mental health needs

- multi-agency approaches and routes of referral

- contradictory constructions of young people

- consultation and participation.

Achievements of First Strategy

The first strategy aimed to:

- develop an agreed tiered approach to service provision

- appoint specific staff, strengthen teams, develop training (including joint training) and improve accommodation

- focus on services that took account of young people who experience learning disabilities, physical disabilities and/or are young offenders

- improve emergency arrangements.

The local children's rights organisation report called for:

- the service to be renamed and more comfortable/welcoming services provided

- more choice regarding workers, more child-centred services and more work to be done on the quality of the relationship between young people and workers

- complaints procedures and suggestion boxes

- young people's groups and representatives

- advocates, self-referral and better confidentiality.

The first strategy led to a number of outcomes. These included the development of:

- a strategy implementation and stakeholders group

- a needs assessment by the local university and an audit of services linked to the National CAMHS Mapping Exercise and local performance indicators

- staff training and organisational development by the local children's rights organisation

- specific frontline projects (e.g. development of school based provision such as the Education CAMHS Workers)

- a parents and carers group

- new CAMHS teams in specific areas

- a transition service delivery model (16/17 year olds) from CAMHS to adult services

- appointment of a CAMHS strategy implementation manager

- appointment of Primary Mental Health Workers (PMHW)

- expansion of provision for children and young people experiencing the looked after system, post adoption service and trauma/abuse

- multi-disciplinary teams in specific local high-incidence areas

- a new clinical base for specialist CAMHS

- a CAMHS Learning and Development Strategy Manager and increased training opportunities

- a CAMHS Commissioning Group.

A number of reports outlined the successes achieved by the first strategy with particular mention being given to increased staff training, clearer advice/support for parents/children, better filtering of referrals, greater liaison between services and clearer pathways in/out of specialist care.

It was possible to conclude that the new strategy offered a realistic opportunity for further improvements in services if the aim to develop more integrated service provision was supported by processes that enable different stakeholders to consider how their different constructions of childhood, different traditions concerning referral and assessment and different approaches to treatment/ therapy impacted on decision-making processes.

Activity

Consider the context of this work. Very often there is a process of constant change in local authorities. By looking back at different reports and charting processes of change, it was hoped that a clearer picture could be obtained of how to plan the new strategy. How regularly are you able to review your service? Can you in your workplace or placement look back across different reviews and see if a consistent picture can become clear. In some cases the same unaddressed issue comes up in each review – why is that? What steps can be taken to ensure that such issues are addressed much earlier?

Estimating the Prevalence of Child and Adolescent Mental Health Issues

The local reports raised issues concerning how to develop more efficient systems for assessing need. They suggested that many professionals are not well placed to do this (e.g. they identified problems with the knowledge of 45% of local GPs). There was a difficulty when assessing needs because there was no clear understanding of what need was and/or who was best placed to assess need.

In three local reports, various types of staff (health and education) reported 18%, 14–20% and 20–26% of children as having mental health needs. The local university report drawing from national averages suggested that 9.5% of children might have a 'disorder'. The Office of National Statistics figures suggested that the population of children with mental health issues in the local area could range from 14% to 23%. As such it was possible to estimate that service needs would range from 14% to 26% of children depending on the context of the local sub-area (e.g. instances would be higher in more deprived wards).

In the main, these reports employed individual assessment scales and models (e.g. Goodman's, SDQ, Connors, Achenbach, etc.) that were not necessarily recognised by professionals from backgrounds outside of psychology, e.g. social work, family work, community education, counselling, teaching, childcare and early education. Similarly, a number of reports referred to NICE guidelines that tend to privilege professional views over those of parents, children and young people. In particular, questions were raised of how to assess mental health issues in early years settings. This brought up issues concerning how and if a solid, local and agreed professional notion of assessment could be developed that involved joint assessment across agencies.

The reports demonstrated a need for greater multi-professional collaboration during assessment and the need to give more consideration to the question of who is best placed to make comment on issues of assessment that affect children of different ages, young people and families. They also highlighted the planning difficulties for those wishing to predict joint commissioning needs and provide timely/accessible services. For example, the local children's rights organisation reported that around one-third of children and young people who encountered mental health issues did not know what help was available. This suggested that whatever the prevalence, services may only have been engaging with two-thirds of potential cases.

Some authors encourage us to question the way we assess children (e.g. particularly in relation to ADHD) (Davis, 2006). The development of the new social studies of childhood has resulted in a huge explosion of literature on research with children (Davis, 2006; Tisdall et al., 2009). This literature raises questions concerning ethics, roles and tools that are best employed by adults to interpret the meanings of children's behaviour. A number of authors highlight the requirement for adults to be reflexive when interpreting children's behaviour (Davis, 1998, 2006). This requires a rigorous qualitative approach where practitioners question their own professional and personal preconceptions. It also requires adults to observe children over a sustained time period in a large variety of social contexts and consider how their behaviour relates to the cultural and political contexts in which the children live (Davis, 2006). Davis (2006) argues that there is little evidence that the adults who are tasked with diagnosing children's mental health issues have been trained in reflexive techniques and know how to develop participatory approaches to working with children. Indeed, there is evidence that some adults who work with disabled children fail to consistently take account of children's own views or question their long-held assumptions and privilege medical model assumptions rather than strengths based approaches (Davis and Watson, 2000; Davis et al., 2000).

Activity

Consider the way that you have been asked to assess children. Do you use short-term tick-box approaches? Or do you have sufficient time to carry out observations in different settings, talk to the range of professionals involved and speak to parents, siblings and the children themselves?

Multi-Agency Approaches to Referral and Assessment

The local university report identified a range of referral routes including:

- a route involving GPs, paediatricians and CAMHS

- a route involving educational psychologists and behaviour support

- a route involving educational welfare officers, school nurses and health visitors

- a route involving Youth Offending Teams and social services

- a route involving STEP (a Tier 2 team who work with children/young people who have experienced significant trauma with ongoing impact)[1] and CAMHS

- a route involving STEP, social services and CAMHS.

The local children's right's organisation report demonstrated that children and young people turned to a range of people for help and advice, for example doctors, friends, teachers, work colleagues, help lines and advice centres. When considering issues of early intervention, young people felt that the new strategy should enable them to have easier access to people they could trust to provide help and that they should be able to choose who that was:

> You know like in school you might go to the school nurse, if you have got a school counsellor you might go to your school counsellor. If you are in college you might go to like the counselling service or whatever, like student service they have in the college. But you might have a good relationship with a social worker. You don't know until you try it out.

> It's the person, just because they have got some kind of title on them doesn't make them like a better person to talk to.

There appears to be a need for clearer and more creative pathways of referral. The children and young people were clear that these processes should not involve compulsion:

> It doesn't work when you are being told that you *have* to do something, when you are not in a state to actually do that thing.

> That's a really good point actually, 'cause … some of the other stuff that's been brought up, the school nurse stuff, is that a lot of young people have been referred to a school nurse, or have been referred to other people by like a professional, and not told about it, and so they don't understand why they have been sent and they have not given their permission to be sent, and so by the time they get there they are like I don't care, I don't want to be here, I don't know why I am here, and you can basically get lost, I don't want to talk to you.

> My support worker and I know that when I am down and I am told to go to that meeting I am not happy at all. They have never done that (forced a meeting) but if you don't feel well or you are not happy enough coming, you shouldn't be forced to.

The local university report argued that services needed to engage with all the individuals who had some involvement in a situation where mental health issues had arisen, for example child, family, school, primary care, CAMHS professional, and that there was a need for earlier intervention. Some young people supported this view:

> And I think another important point, I think that if people are more into families before things start going wrong, like the families that are having more trouble which is quite often poorer families, then you wouldn't get so far as to have to like use health services. Some children get fed breakfast when their parents aren't feeding them breakfast, and although that helps that's not everything.

This quote demonstrated the ability of the young person to articulate the requirement for service based on early intervention. It also highlights the social aspects of well-being. This issue can easily be overlooked. For example, there was criticism of Tier 4 acute services that were based in locations where young people became isolated from their friends and family. It was concluded that more attention should be given in the new strategy to the aim of enabling children and young people to access local flexible services. This finding is similar to that described by Glenny and Roaf (2008) which suggested that children and young people need support at early stages, that there should be greater communication between home and school and that we should provide greater support for families who are struggling with a range of issues.

It was also concluded that the Tier 4 service should be made more accessible by providing young people, their friends and their families with more information on the nature of Tier 4 services, a picture of the building (prior to admission) and maps of bus routes to the service.

Similarly, young people did not welcome some professional therapeutic techniques:

> Yeah 'cause I had a psychologist once and he refused to be called by anything else, he had to be called a child psychologist otherwise he actually shouted at the receptionist once because she didn't call him that, and it's more about his titles than what he did, and it was obvious because he just didn't give a shit about me or listening to us, he just used to twiddle his thumbs and go, 'and how did that make you feel', I hate them, I hate them people who just keep saying, 'and how did you feel about that' ...

Indeed, many young people criticised the 'neutral' approach to therapy:

> Professional people just sit there and look at you as if you are mad, they don't comfort you because they're not allowed to. Like friends can make you feel better because they can comfort you.

> They don't have to cuddle you to make you feel better, they could do it in another way but just actually make you feel like they care, rather than you're a problem.

This suggests that evaluation of individual interactions between children and professionals should be carried out to enable young people to quickly identify inappropriate forms of assessment and treatment.

It is possible to conclude that greater consideration should be given to opening up discussion concerning professional conflict about identification, assessment and treatment. For example, some local health reports raised issues concerning the causes of children's hyperactivity. These lacked consideration of how hyperactivity could be related to environmental and socio-cultural issues such as the educational system (e.g. national testing), teacher methods, or interaction with peer group (see Davis [2006] for further discussion). Indeed, young people pointed out that teachers and schools often caused the factors that led to them being stressed:

> Aye but if you have bullying from teachers ... Like my maths teacher just picked on me the whole time, like in lessons and that, I don't like it when they do that. Teachers are like well protected really, aren't they. They can like shout and scream at you. What can you do if a teacher is bullying you?

> Well the only thing you could say, the only thing you would do is to make others aware of it, is to actually have the student report it, but who is going to believe the student against the teacher.

> I think teachers have to actually give children and young people some power in the schools because they don't actually have any at all.

It was possible to conclude that the shift to a more integrated approach that was aimed for in the CAMHS strategy should be underpinned by processes of planning that showed greater consideration of:

- children and young people's perspectives of the different professions and professionals that make up integrated service

- the appropriateness of different processes of assessment, referral and treatment

- the need to involve children and young people in discussion concerning early intervention and to provide easier access to people they can trust

- the need to ensure that young people understand the referral processes and why they are being asked to engage with a specific professional or service.

Chapter 2 highlighted the need to build strong relationships in integrated services – this includes strong relationships with parents and children. A number of authors report a need for non-judgemental relationships when working with children (Rixon, 2008b). Yet, children and young people critique neutral approaches.

Activity

Can you work out the difference between being non-judgemental and neutral? In the previous chapter we saw that it involved working with people at 'the person' level. It is clear from the comments above that these young people judged professionals (and the effectiveness of the service) on the basis of whether they cared, were trustworthy, enabled choice and took time to explain processes. How effective are you at these skills? Do you have values and can you show levels of commitment that will enable you to gain the respect of the people you work with? Chapter 2 also highlighted the need for difficult issues to be raised in processes of developing and providing integrated services. How good are you at raising issues with colleagues? A central aspect of professionalism is having the confidence to review your practice with colleagues. How often do you review your own work and are you involved in reviewing the work of others? What is done with the issues that are raised during review?

Contradictory Constructions of Children and Young People

The findings concerning conflicting models of assessment, referral and support were underpinned by contradictory ideas concerning children and young people. For example, one local health report discussed solutions such as circle time and cognitive behavioural therapy without making clear to their audience that these two approaches were based on completely conflicting philosophies concerning children (the first philosophy perceived the adult's role to be to facilitate learning/dialogue, the second perceived the adult's role to be to ensure children knew the correct way to behave).

Similarly, little awareness was shown of young people's own critiques of peer group approaches such as circle time:

> Yeah because there wouldn't be enough trust there, because you wouldn't know if you could trust them, and they could tell anyone in the school about your problem.

> Yeah, like when it's a professional they could lose their job if they told someone, another young person, they have got nothing to lose by it.

The local health report can be strongly contrasted with the Strategic Partnership Agenda that aimed to:

- identify partner agencies

- strengthen communication

- raise awareness of a breadth of causal factors

- share analysis of hard evidence

- enable participation of children, parents and young people

- plan intervention

- link emotional well-being to family support, child development and community prosperity

- develop future provision through children's centres, schools/extended services and community services.

At the centre of this new agenda was the idea that children and young people could participate in processes of service development. For example, the local university report, a report into 'Developing the Workforce', the local children's rights organisation report and several presentations by CAMHS mangers at stakeholders' events all highlighted the benefits of children/family centres, outlined the usefulness of holistic approaches, promoted the notion that services should challenge social exclusion, and underlined the value of children and young people producing solutions for their own life issues.

These reports promoted the idea that children and young people are agents who can actively make choices, enter into dialogue with service providers and be central to identifying the solutions to their life problems. Yet, there is a big difference between this perspective and the somewhat negative perspective of the three psychology reports on prevalence and the local health report that tended to take the position that the local problems of children and young people needed greater funding of interventions from expensive health and psychology professionals.

It was possible to conclude that different professionals within the multi-agency setting needed to be clearer about the different ways that they characterised children and young people and, therefore, assessed and treated mental heath issues. For example, the local university report suggested that there was considerable evidence to demonstrate the effectiveness of multi-systemic assessment yet some professionals were found to employ individualised strategies that they had not been formally trained to carry out (e.g. some professionals instituted Cognitive Behavioural Therapy (CBT) on the back of very informal training).

The new strategy aimed to achieve greater clarity by identifying key outcomes by which to assess the effectiveness of CAMHS. It aimed to include the views of parents, children and young people at the centre of this assessment and to ensure that services were accessible and inclusive. The children's rights organisation report demonstrated that this process had already begun. However, neither the first nor second strategy demonstrated an understanding of the complexity of such processes and the need for the different professionals that make up the integrated service to have the opportunity to consider their different professional and personal constructions of childhood.

Activity

Reflect on your perspective on working with children. Do you believe you are the expert who will solve their problems, or do you believe that you are good at listening to children and enabling them to take charge of solving their life problems? Do you see the children you work with as victims or as people who can make choices, have strengths and plan their own future? Have you ever carried out an assessment and not been able to write down anything positive about the child, their family or their community? Did you ask the child what they thought their strengths were, who the people were that they trusted and who they would prefer to work with?

Consultation and Participation: Involving Children and Young People

The previous strategy had aimed to create comprehensive information systems and systems of evaluation, monitoring and quality assurance. The strategy also connected with the development of NSF standards that highlighted the need for children, young people, parents and/or carers to be consulted about the development of services, or services/agencies to work in partnership and services to respond to the needs of a diverse population (DOH, 1999).

The first strategy led the children's rights organisation to carry out work with children and young people on how services could be more responsive to their needs. This work suggested that the good aspects of CAMHS centred on the opportunities the services offered for children and young people to talk about feelings, the opportunity to talk to people confidentially and the feeling that staff do their best for the children and young people they engage with. However, children and young people also felt that CAMHS could be improved and were particularly critical of counsellors that talked down to them, stared at them and failed to keep appointments. Specific issues that had improved since the first strategy included choices, staff training, efforts to reduce stigma and attempts to increase the availability of help. However, a number of young people were keen that the new strategy should specifically target the role of teachers and other professionals in schools:

> School staff should be trained better in improving student/teacher relationships. Where the student requires confidentiality there should also be more approachable people in schools who can develop relationships for counselling.

At present, approaches to staff training have been centred on better information regarding mental health issues, reduction of stigma, early identification, prevention, etc. It was possible to conclude that this training needs to engage more closely with children and young people's concepts of need and to include young people as trainers:

> Give them [staff] better training, training by young people or people chosen by young people. The strategy says give them more training but doesn't say who's doing the training.

This issue was being addressed by staff development training carried out by the local children's rights organisations. It was hoped that joint training would encourage a conceptual shift that would, in turn, enable the new strategy to move young people from experiencing isolated consultation projects to being at the heart of decision-making concerning service development. Children and young people argued that there was a need to link participation to outcomes, dialogue and change. In particular, children and young people wanted to be at the centre of processes to agree the indicators that would be used to define the success of the strategy.

The new strategy set out the role of the commissioning group and specifically tasked the commissioning group with ensuring there was appropriate consultation to enable planning and development and that the views of children, young people, parents and/or carers were an integral part of the commissioning and performance management framework.

It was argued that any joint assessment process should work through the differences between young people's and professionals' views of what causes stress and what issues impact on mental well-being. It was also suggested that the new strategy should be judged on how easy it became for children and young people to put forward their own solutions to their life issues and how quickly those suggestions were acted upon.

In was concluded that there was a need to develop local forms of joint assessment that involved a range of stakeholders' perspectives including the child and non-psychology/health professionals. The CAMHS service had aspirations to be more joined up and to involve inter-agency working. It was concluded that for this to be achieved different professional allegiances to different forms of assessment and treatment would have to be explored and the power relations within different service settings would have to be better understood.

The young people could differentiate between successful and unsuccessful participation events:

> Well obviously the adults had more experience, because some of them were doctors, some of them were GPs, and some of them were like teachers and that, and they had way more experience about dealing with like emotional well-being, do you know what I mean ... but they were all comparing their own experiences with each other like, 'I work in this school' ...

> The way they are talking to each other is they just like intimidate you and make it out as if you are a kid and you don't know anything. When I told them stuff about ... that had happened at school to me and stuff that was relevant to what we were talking about, they were shocked, do you know what I mean, and I think it made them realise well we will stop talking amongst ourselves and we will like involve you, because I was going on about how teachers didn't understand when the school student was like in a situation, depressed and that, and why they were being distracted from their school work and that and they didn't realise that, and they just stopped and they were like well we will listen to you 'cause they were too busy going on about themselves. Do you know what I mean?

This raised an important issue of how participatory processes should be organised to enable children and young people to engage with staff in various services. The young people above felt that they could have organised the participatory processes better themselves, if they were able to have organised it from the start and actively organised each stage of the process. Indeed, they were keen to be given the opportunity to organise any future events to discuss the new strategy.

This finding also indicates that the ground rules for engagement between staff and children/young people need to be made clearer. For example, the young people above were also critical of the fact that local authority strategies were written in a language that made them inaccessible to non-professionals, children and young people.

A number of young people pointed out that there is a difference between 'consultation' and actual participation in decision-making. They also felt that processes of participation would be improved if staff did not wear suits to participation events and did not assume that their qualifications made them more important than other people:

> I think the way they are trained, like how they have to go and get a degree and all of that, kind of teaches them that they should know all the answers and so then they think well what's the point in me getting these qualifications if they are going to listen to you who has no qualifications. And I think that's probably the biggest problem. It is harder to just listen to somebody else and do what they want, rather than do it your own way.

This issue suggests we need to consider the power relations within processes of consultation, participation, evaluation and review. Indeed, more work needs to be done on informing professionals of the key principles and ethics of participatory working. For example, Lansdown (2001: 11) suggests that the characteristics of effective and genuine participation are that:

- the issue is of real relevance to children themselves

- the project has the capacity to make a difference in the long term

- adequate time and resources are made available

- realistic expectations are made of children (e.g. clear goals and targets are agreed with children)

- the projects are underpinned by the values of trust, respect and equity

- training/support is provided to the adults, children and young people who participate so they can contribute to the planning/delivery of the project.

It may also be important to convince staff of the benefits of participatory approaches. For example, it has been argued that participation benefits children and young people because it:

- aids their identity and personal and social development

- enables them to feel empowered and develop their sense of responsibility

- improves their decision-making, confidence, self-esteem and independence

- develops their co-operation, sharing, discussion, debating, listening, planning, negotiating and problem-solving skills

- enables interaction with other children of different ages, gender, ethnicity, locality or identity

- increases their experience of working to timescales, deadlines and targets

- leads them to develop a heightened awareness of democracy, diversity, social justice, equity and human rights

- promotes their protection from abuse/neglect by developing avenues of dialogue between themselves and adults

- enables them to contribute to the protection and development of their own communities

- leads them to increase their future job prospects, achieve their aspirations and have fun.

(Hogan, 2003; Kirby, 1999; Kirby and Bryson, 2002; Kjorholt, 2002; Lansdown, 2001; Sinclair and Franklin, 2000)

The benefits of participation are also related to issues within workplaces. It is argued that individual staff, organisations or services all have something to gain when children and young people are encouraged and supported to participate in decision-making processes. The benefits may be that:

- Children will influence the design and delivery of the service, making it more relevant to the service users and therefore more receptive, relevant and efficient

- Children will introduce new and innovative ideas that boost staff morale, productivity and effectiveness

- The involvement of children will help to ensure that resources are targeted more effectively

- Involvement in participatory processes can contribute to processes of staff continual professional development.

(Hogan, 2003; Kirby and Bryson, 2002)

Yet, participation should not be viewed as an end in itself or as the perfect solution to problems of service development. For example, many participatory projects have little impact on public decision-making (Kirby and Bryson, 2002). It has been suggested that participatory processes often fail because they:

- are selective in the types of children they allow to participate

- only provide adults with decision-making positions

- do not create long-term dialogue between practitioners, service mangers and children

- only involve tokenistic consultation, where children and young people are asked for their views but never know if consideration of their views has resulted in service change

- alienate children and young people because they do not fulfil the promises made at the start of the process.

(Borland et al., 2001; Dorrian et al., 2001; Tisdall and Davis, 2004)

In a survey of local authorities, it was found that only 12% of councils provided councillors with training on involving young people in service development. Many decision-makers were resistant to 'training' on any issue-based topic, including (but not specifically) youth issues (Kirby and Bryson, 2002). Other writers have suggested that establishing dialogue with key workers in a specific service is related to more complex reasons than a lack of training. They suggest that the rhetoric of participation is 'highly seductive' but that its implementation in, for example, social care settings, requires skill and commitment from individual social workers (Gilligan, 2000). Prout et al. (2006) argued that people's ability to participate is related to whether they have the necessary resources, motivation, opportunities and context. Elsewhere, barriers to participation are linked to issues of skills, commitment and a lack of space for adults and children to discuss solutions (Moss and Petrie, 2002). As we have seen, Moss and Petrie (2002) argue that we need numerous long-term and short-term ways to promote 'discursive space' between adults, children and young people. These spaces need to be established in everyday settings such as schools, community centres and leisure/entertainment venues. They need to be structured in a way that enables participants to foster quick responses to everyday issues.

It was concluded that the continued involvement of the local children's rights organisation would be a crucially important aspect of the implementation of the new CAMHS. It was also concluded that different forms of participation should be developed at different levels of service provision. The development of a specific participation strategy allied to the training already provided by the children's rights organisation could better clarify contemporary practice for staff.

Activity

Consider whether you have the confidence to develop participatory approaches. The young people in this study suggested that some professionals had very poor communication skills. Are you aware of the different children's organisations that work in your field? If you are a manager can you work with them to increase the skills of your staff or organisation? If you work in a local authority, is there a participation officer in your local area? What training structures exist that might enable you to develop skills around the issue of participation? If you are a student, how participatory are your tutors? Very often in schools and universities, people teach participation but cannot demonstrate it – have you had experience of that? Do you have the professionalism to raise such issues with the people who run your programme? Most professional programmes are required to include service users in their development – does your university/college do this?

Discussion: Defining Mental Health Needs and Concepts of Support

The local children' rights organisation report, that outlined the views of children and young people, identified a range of services provided by professionals including specialist CAMHS, drop-in services, counselling, health education groups, family therapy, child protection/social services, accommodation, information, play therapy, group therapy and medication. The report also stated that children and young people had different reasons for using services. For example:

- To help them change something about themselves as individuals
- To help their family
- To get information
- To receive understanding
- To enable them to talk to other people.

Their report outlined a number of key issues for children and young people:

- It linked a sense of well-being with social issues such as money, friends, having someone to turn to, stress at school/college, family relationships and bereavement.
- It also linked a sense of well-being to ideas of self, health issues, feelings of isolation, depression, unhappiness, pressure, and dealing with past experiences.

(Continued)

(Continued)

The numerous reports into CAMHS in the local area demonstrated that there were a variety of professional positions on how mental health issues should be identified and treated. These included:

- Approaches based on individual assessment and treatment (e.g. medication, self-regulation, relaxation, parenting classes or behaviourist therapy)
- Approaches based on changing the social conditions in which young people live (e.g. through financial support, addressing bullying in schools, provision of family support/therapy)
- Approaches that attempted to be preventative by working at an early stage with Children's Centres, communities, schools, extended schools and families
- Approaches that attempt to be preventative by educating teachers, parents, children, young people and peer groups
- Approaches that combined some or all of the above.

The problems with assessing prevalence raise questions about how we assess children's service requirements. For example, should children's service requirements be assessed through individualised approaches, ecological models, multi-agency approaches or holistic strengths based models?

Individualised Approaches

These approaches consider the individual child's pathology and judge children against normative criteria related to developmental age and stage. For example, very often they are aligned to practices where professionals position themselves as neutral but then adopt techniques which 'train' children or ask children to train themselves into behaving 'appropriately'. Such approaches have been heavily criticised for lacking an understanding of cultural diversity and imposing on children adult ideas of what children should be (Alderson, 2000). They have also been criticised for failing to fully assess the social context of children's behaviour, for example many of these approaches employ simplistic tick-box scales that take a few minutes to assess a child's 'problem' (Davis, 2006).

Ecological Models

These approaches are based on the work of Bronfenbrenner (1989) and show awareness of the issues outside of the individual child. The child is perceived to be at the centre of a series of rings that include their immediate friends, school and neighbours, wider structures such as school policies and local services, and issues related to national culture, government and the media. These approaches are much more complex than individualised approaches, however there is still a tendency for adults to decide what the solutions are to children's problems, for the politics of

(Continued)

(Continued)

child/adult relations to be overlooked and for family problems relating to poor services to be ignored (Davis, 2007; Smith and Davis, 2010).

Multi-Agency Approaches

These approaches aim to ensure that no one professional defines children's 'problems' or the solutions to their life issues. They aim to enable dialogue between parents, children and service providers, earlier identification of issues and 'joined up' approaches to service provision. For example, Moss and Petrie (2002) suggest that we need to move from thinking about children's services as a set of adult rules, norms, principles and rationales to basing children's services on contingent relationships that enable surprise, doubt and uncertainty. They argue that this shift does not require adults who work with children and young people to totally give up their agenda (that might include specific pre-determined outcomes), rather, it requires adults to balance their aspirations with those of children and young people. Moss and Petrie (2002) suggest that local authorities need to create 'discursive space' that enables adults and children to contest understandings, values, practices and knowledges, promoting different ways of thinking about ethics, relationships, practices and structures. They contrast this approach with those underpinned by techniques of managerialism that aim to 'process' children through services. They argue that such approaches close off discursive spaces by employing techniques of rationing, targeting and priority setting.

In other countries these approaches have involved an appreciation of cultural differences and consideration of how other cultures define family, parenting and childhood. At the centre of this approach is a critique of how service providers have traditionally viewed the abilities of families and children (Moore et al., 2005).

Politically Nuanced Holistic Models

These approaches have been developed in the field of family therapy where there has been a shift from hierarchical approaches that assume that the medical professional knows best to a position where (in a similar way to the multi-agency approach) service users are assumed to be the expert on their own lives and professionals are believed to be experts at facilitating processes of resolution. Family therapy has shifted from Freudian approaches that aim to identify what is wrong with individuals, to viewing families as a whole unit (Smith and Davis, 2010).

This shift in how we now approach the life difficulties of families and children has led professionals to reconsider the nature of family support. For example, Gilligan (2000: 15) describes three different types of family support including universal welfare services that support all families (developmental), specialist community based provision that is targeted at

(Continued)

(Continued)

those perceived to be most in need or in crisis (compensatory) and family support which aims to support family resilience by promoting children's competence and encouraging their integration into the family or community unit (protective).

Smith (2007) concludes that it is possible to develop a model that crosses all three types of family support, that is underpinned by strong partnerships between professionals and that has clear agreements concerning joint assessment. She stresses the importance of parents, children and young people accessing the most appropriate solutions and not simply ones that come about because of the routes they take through the system.

Conclusion

This chapter confirms the work of Christensen (1999) that considers the cultural processes of health, arguing that illness is a distinctive social event interpreted in a number of ways by different social actors. She has demonstrated the 'here and now' of children's constructs of health and argued that children's accounts of health are characterised by discussions of social interactions, social positions and social processes that include themselves interacting with other people (e.g. friends, parents, grandparents and professionals). In childhood studies many writers have encouraged us to investigate the interconnectedness of the body to social places and the importance of understanding the role of social relations in different social locations (Dyck, 1999; Stables and Smith, 1999; Valentine, 1999). In this project most of the young people highlight the importance of the social as well as the organisational aspects of mental health services. This leads to the conclusion that when integrated services do not confront conceptual differences and professional vested interests, parents, teachers, counsellors, psychologists and medical professionals can fall into the trap of labelling children and young people rather than making their wishes central to service development and building strong, supportive and trustful relationships.

---

[1]A definition of tiers: Tier 1: provided by non-mental health professionals; Tier 2: provided by CAMHS community/primary care professionals; Tier 3: a specialist service for more complex referrals provided by a local multi-agency team; and Tier 4: specialist teams/units usually serving more than one area for the most serious referrals.

6

Participation, Disabled Young People and Integrated Children's Services

This chapter includes a short summary of a report written with John Hogan and Kathryn Burns (Davis et al., 2006). Many thanks go to John and Kathryn for enabling me to use the summary.

Chapter Overview

This chapter considers writing in disability and childhood studies that promotes the involvement of disabled children in service development. It discusses the findings from a specific project that aimed to build relationships between service providers and disabled young people. It also considers the project's problems, whether the project enabled disabled children and young people's views to influence policy making/service delivery, and the tensions between individual children's rights based approaches and the notion that children and families should not be worked with in isolation from each other.

It is concluded that whilst policies based on individual rights are useful because they act as signposts for standards we should all follow, they tend to reflect outdated 'needs' based ideas of service provision. It is also argued that strengths based approaches require service providers to move away from only considering impairment needs – to also investigating how provision can address the social issues of disability such as poverty, appropriate housing, access to transport, the ability to build relationships and opportunities for employment.

In January 2004 I was involved in a project in England that aimed to develop sustained engagement between disabled young people and local authority services (Davis and Hogan, 2004; Davis et al., 2006). The methods used to carry out the Communications 2004 project are discussed elsewhere (see Davis and Hogan, 2004). The project included resources to employ four disabled young people. The template for this process had originally been suggested by young people during a year-long project entitled Diversity and Difference that had asked young people what they wanted to change about local services and how they would like to engage with their local council (see Davis and Hogan, 2004).

The four young people were employed to carry out a number of tasks including:

- peer research with children/young people involved in children's fund projects

- discussion days with disabled and deaf children/young people

- communication events with 'decision makers' from local organisations and services.

The project was not only based on the participatory principles to be found in childhood studies but was also underpinned by emancipatory principles from disability studies. In disability studies it is argued that disabled people should take an active role in projects about their lives; lead projects themselves or work in equal partnership with those who lead projects; be consulted about the planning of projects; and be able to alter the course of projects (Davis and Hogan, 2004).

At the centre of emancipatory principles is the idea that projects are only worthwhile if they lead to real changes in the life conditions of disabled people and that those who support such projects should aim to facilitate processes where disabled people are able to achieve self-emancipation (Davis, 2000; Davis and Hogan, 2004). This distinction between emancipation and self-emancipation is an important one.

Emancipation and participation can often be seen as a gift or token provided at the behest of the powerful (e.g. politicians, service managers, teachers, etc.). Disability studies writers are very cynical about such power relationships and are keen to ensure that emancipatory processes do more than simply boost the reputations and careers of such people (see Davis, 2000). Similarly, the project raised ethical issues. The ethical issues were: informed consent, confidentiality and protection (Davis, 1998). The Communications project was underpinned by the belief that processes of consultation should be respectful and fair to the children, parents and young people and that they should avoid placing participants in stressful positions (Alderson, 1995; Beresford, 1997; Morrow and Richards, 1996). Every effort was made to ensure that the participants understood what the project involved and that participation was voluntary (Ross and Ross, 1984). Information was provided concerning the confidentiality of their responses and a written indication of consent was sought from each participant and/or their guardian (Beresford, 1997). Consent was reaffirmed on a continuous basis throughout discussions and every effort was made to ensure that participants did not suffer harm when discussing sensitive issues (Beresford, 1997; Morrow and Richards, 1996).

The Findings of the Communications 2004 Project

The four young people visited a range of young people and organised a day event attended by over 100 disabled children and young people. The views of these children and young people were separated into three distinct themes: 'what I require to be included'; 'what I require to be understood'; and 'what I want to say to decision makers'. The following quotes are taken from a much longer report that was presented to decision makers in public and voluntary organisations in the local area (Davis et al., 2006).

'What I Require to be Included'

To answer questions, company [meaning companionship], friends [skills to make friends], favourite things, pictures [to understand things].

Good toys to play with, packed lunch, respect, no bullying, to learn.

Transport, and P.A. to help me with all my needs. I also need to know if the places I visit are wheelchair accessible.

More choices – free transport and safe transport.

To be able to play games and jigsaws with other people, I would like to play with other people from other schools.

I want a friend to play football with me.

The children and young people had quite diverse things that they felt could address inclusion. They made suggestions in two rough categories – one regarding physical things (e.g. food, toys, transport) and the other related to feelings/relationships (e.g. safety, trust and respect). However, it should not be assumed that this summary means that there was one collective voice or that disabled children are a homogeneous group.

'What I Require to be Understood'

Transport to places – I need support – I need someone to listen – To be careful in the city – We want to be included with other people.

I like to go out with my friend to meet others and have fun so I need adults to understand that we don't always need them around.

To be understood – I need people to listen to me about where I want to go.

People to be patient with me, and to give me more time to do what I have to do.

In the main, the young people stressed the need for people to be considerate of their different ways of communicating but they also stressed the need for opportunities to be themselves.

'What I Want to Say to Decision Makers'

The majority of young people in our area tend to be ignored when it comes to their lives. I feel that adults think they know best when it comes to making decisions, in my opinion, 'they don't' all of the time. You can learn something new every day. Who says it can't be from a young person. Listen to our views and I assure you, you will learn something.

Free transport because my mom doesn't work and can't afford to take all three of us out.

When someone comes to your building is it accessible? Is there someone to communicate with the young person about where to go? Is the lift working?

Disabled and Deaf young people want to be included in events outside of school and want the same opportunities as other young people.

Organisations need to have an access budget so that support can be provided. Opportunities need to be given to young people so that they can build their confidence.

Ask young people their views and then keep them informed as to what you are doing with what they have told you.

These findings were similar to the previous Diversity and Difference report that found that children and young people wanted much more disability awareness events and processes in local authority services (e.g. social services, transport and education); improved access to public transport; greater opportunities to experience transition to work; and greater inclusion in education, leisure, play and sport (Davis et al., 2006).

Activity

Chapter 2 discussed writing that promoted the involvement of children and families in integrated service development (Foley, 2008; Leathard, 2003b). It was suggested that such approaches required strong relationships to be built with both parents and children (Glenny and Roaf, 2008). Can you find out how people enable disabled children and young people

(Continued)

(Continued)

to influence service development in your area? Do they work with them in isolation or with their peer group and family?

How effective are you at listening to disabled children? Davis and Watson (2000) and Davis et al. (2000) indicated that some professionals assume that children who do not 'talk' do not think. Such writing illustrates the need for professionals to question their own presumptions about childhood and disability as well as the need to assume that disabled children are competent to make decisions and the need to presume that disabled children's views change over time. Have you had training on different ways of communicating? If you have gaps in your knowledge, could you discuss this with local professionals who could exchange knowledge with you (e.g. speech and language therapists)?

Did the Communications 2004 Project Influence Policy Making?

The four young people presented (at a final project event) the findings from the project to staff, managers and senior managers of public services and voluntary organisations. The adult participants were asked to respond to what they had heard. Many responded by talking about new initiatives that were already in place to improve things for Disabled/Deaf children and young people. These included:

- The development of inclusive play opportunities

- The development of a participation strategy for projects within the local Children's Fund

- The development of a strategic partnership and plan for service providers in the local authority

- The restructuring of the provision of short breaks and occupational therapy services

- The opportunity for children and young people to work with disabled adults in organisations

- The development of a young people's participation group in health

- The commissioning of organisations to develop the provision of independent living and to expand direct payments

- The work of local primary care trusts to develop accessible information and disability equality training.

Many of these initiatives had emerged in response to the previous Diversity and Difference report. This enabled the 'decision makers' to demonstrate the importance they placed on children and young people's views. Many of the adult participants made pledges to change other aspects of their services/ organisations. Following the event, they were contacted to ascertain their perspective of the experience. For the most part, they stated that they believed that the event had achieved its primary aim: to inform people in a clear, enthusiastic, effective, inspiring and humorous way. They praised the team-work, effort and perseverance of the young people and gave examples of where the event had already influenced their practice:

> One of my functions is to give out the Council's money and look at how money could be spent differently to enable disabled children to access the same things that other children want. Hopefully next year and in years to come, money previously used for specific services will be used to help disabled children and young people to access things they want. Transport is part of that. Direct payments are good as it gives you opportunities to access services you want.

> I would love to say that the event did not influence our practice. However, it has pointed us in a few directions we may not have gone in, thinking about travel arrangements and the accessibility in terms of knowing the driver, communicating throughout the journey etc.

> The event has encouraged us to think more creatively about the participation of the young people we work with. We have already changed our service level agreements to reinforce the participation agenda ...

Service Providers' Problems with the Participatory Process

The same people who praised the final event also demonstrated a sense of frustration with the process. They felt that more councillors and more of the most senior service managers should have been at the event. They also felt that the findings from the young people's work should have been disseminated to a broader audience and that steps should have been taken to enable greater involvement of children and young people on key strategic committees within the local authority.

> We need to listen to young people, take on board what they say and give them a response. We need to produce project progress reports so they know what we are doing and where we are going, at the moment there is little or no flexibility to involve children in the process of making decisions.

> There is still work being done to see that the messages shared at the second event get into the hands of those who make the top decisions. Stimulating policy and service change can take years and can also be done on various levels. I am sure the first stages of making people aware of the issues was achieved, but there is a cynical response with regards to whether policies and services will be changed due to the fact that the issues aren't new.

You need to be more proactive re your links to the change agenda in disabled children's services. Otherwise your impact remains at the margins. You want to be at the forefront of bringing fundamental change to this local authority but you are not making your presence felt where it needs to be felt. I can't see the impact on the strategic decision making, where has been the follow up? You need to find out where the main strategic meetings are and get young people involved. That requires you to work differently and also requires your training of the young people to be reconsidered to enable them to participate effectively. They have to get behind the doors and at the tables. If you don't achieve this you won't bring the change you want to see. Get it into the bloodstream of what is happening across agencies and into the decision-making forums.

Interestingly, the final manager did not see it as his/her role to facilitate the young people's participation in committees. She did not perceive herself to be in a position to develop a partnership with the young people and invite them to attend these committees.

> ## Activity
>
> This raises the question of how to develop sustainable participatory processes within local authorities. In the case above the local authority subsequently funded the development of an extensive participation strategy and training of staff. A number of resources exist for auditing how participatory your organisation is. For example, the National Youth Agency has developed a 'Here by Right' tool kit. Have a look on the web and see if you can locate at least two sets of resources that enable organisations to consider issues of participation. How do they compare? What are their key aspects? Do they differentiate between issues of leadership, structure, values, skills and knowledge?
>
> If you are currently working, can you discuss such tools with your line manager (or if you are the line manger with staff) in a team meeting? What strategies do you have for involving children, parents and staff in decision-making in your workplace? How do you evaluate the strategy and judge that it is effective?

Limitations of the Project

From the Communications 2004 project, it is possible to suggest that children and young people are aware of their lack of power, are frustrated by the limitations of participatory processes and wish for a change in the power relations between adults and themselves. The young people on the Communications project stated:

> I was nervous about speaking in public and not to make too many jokes at the council event, but on the day I enjoyed speaking to people about transport, safety and

support. What made it work was the support we got from the project team, the PAs, the school, the transport. On the day people did listen but since then I have read in the paper that support services are still not there for some children and that makes me angry.

From the events I got a greater understanding of children and young people in general and I hope the events change the way things are run. I have a greater understanding now of how hard it is to change something if the people running the service don't want to change, but I think we got the message across to the right people.

I liked the fact that we got paid to do the work, we used our phones and email to organise things and that we got information going round the projects. It was fun going round the projects. I learned that some people wanted to talk to us on their own and that where we talked to people was important. Also, some people take longer to speak than others and you have to learn to listen.

I liked the idea of going out to work and helping the community/organisations. A bad part of the project was the inaccessibility of stairs and cobbled streets. I learned that you should only get in a taxi with people you know. I also learned a lot about making choices and speaking up to difficult people. We told the council to see if they can go out and improve the city. I enjoyed the events and I am very proud of myself.

I enjoyed meeting new people, seeing all the good which people are doing for children, seeing the effect that the projects are having on the children's lives. During the events I played many different roles (registration officer, tour guide, lighting manager, speaker, technical support).

Of particular note was the finding that the young people were frustrated with the time it took services to change. Alderson (1993, 2000) highlights children and young people's ability to make decisions about their lives. She stresses that it is important for those that work with children to reflect on the language they use and the processes by which they engage with children. In particular it was possible to conclude that the timescales of the four young people were at odds with the slower processes within the local authority. A number of writers indicate that services often place disabled children into processes where they develop a learned dependency on service providers (Alderson, 1993; Swain, 1993). For example, very often parents and disabled children are initiated by medical professionals into a medical culture which does not allow space for them to challenge traditional orthodoxy and that fails to recognise conflicts of interests between children, parents and professionals (Avery, 1999; Mayall, 1998; Shakespeare and Watson, 1998). In the main, adults are deemed 'experts' and children are assumed to be unable to put forward their own solutions to their own life problems. This very often leads adults to make decisions about children's lives without consulting them, or assuming that they know what is best for children. Children's problems are identified and resolved by parents and/or professionals and ownership of their own choices is taken away from children (Davis and Watson, 2000). For example, in the health field too much emphasis is placed on adult/parents views at the expense of understanding the things that disabled children and young people want to change about the services that they encounter.

For the most part, this has occurred because a perception exists that disabled children are unable to put forward their own views and that they lack competency and agency (Bricher, 2001; Corker and Davis, 2000; Davis and Watson, 2000; Robinson, 1997; Shakespeare and Watson, 1998). This perception has come about because much of the health based literature concentrates on illustrating the things disabled children cannot do (e.g. how they fail to achieve developmental 'norms'), rather than understanding their skills and abilities (Alderson, 2000; Bricher, 2001; Priestley, 1998; Woodhead and Faulkner, 2000).

It is possible to conclude from the above case study that in some areas such cultures are difficult to challenge and that something needs to be done to speed up the process of service delivery to disabled children and their families. Disabled children are very capable of making their views known when adults make the effort to learn the different ways in which they communicate (Davis et al., 2000). For example, a number of writers have demonstrated that children are capable of making complex medical decisions (Alderson, 1993; Bricher, 2001). Others have urged us to recognise children's knowledge and ability to negotiate health matters (Mayall, 1994, 1996).

Activity

Consider the issues that make organisations more or less responsive to service users. Webster (2000) defines fast-moving organisations as postmodern organisations, defining them as networked, information-rich, de-layered, downsized, lean, boundary-less. It is argued that employees in such organisations are highly skilled, committed, well paid and autonomous (Webster, 2000). The organisations themselves are characterised by processes of quick decision-making, a lack of rigid rules and structures of devolved responsibility (Webster, 2000). Consider the places you have worked in. How flexible were they? Could decisions be made in a responsive way that met people's needs quickly? What incentives do staff have to respond quickly to service users?

Prout et al. (2006) combine social exchange theory, various incentive theories and co-operation theory to argue that there are individual and shared reasons that people take part in local community projects. In particular, they suggest that children will be willing to take part if they are asked, are motivated by the recognition that they have skills to offer and

(Continued)

(Continued)

have the resources needed to be able to take part (e.g. knowledge, equipment, transport, food). Davis and Hogan (2004) indicate the need for participatory processes to be planned properly and to effectively predict/plan the resources that will be required. Can you think of an activity that you have been involved in where you volunteered? How were you treated? Was it easy to get to the place you were working? What support did people provide for you in the workplace? Can you think about this from different children's perspective (e.g. do you need to hire interpreters, pay for their personal assistants to attend or for taxis?) – what things do you need to do to ensure that children can be part of the process of developing the services you work in? What length of time should meetings take? Will you need to provide food and drink?

Discussion: Individual Children's Rights v. Collective Family Support

The National Service Framework (NSF) was developed to set national standards, to drive up their quality, reduce the variability of care and specifically promote an integrated approach to supporting disabled children. A central aim of the NSF was to ensure disabled children gained maximum life chances from educational opportunities, health and social care (DOH, 2002). For example, this aim led to changes such as the Department of Education developing teaching provision in hospitals for disabled children.

The UN Convention on the Rights of the Child Article 12 states that children not only have a right to articulate their opinions with regard to issues that affect them but they also have a right to have these opinions heard. Article 13 declares that the child has a right to seek, receive and impart information and ideas of all kinds (Alderson, 1995; Morrow and Richards, 1996). Various acts, policies and guidance documents suggest that children's opinions should be sought with regard to matters/decisions concerning their welfare (Beresford, 1997). This legislation promotes the objective that children's 'voices' should be listened to by adults who make decisions concerning their lives. However, a number of authors highlight the difficulties that children's service providers encounter when trying to balance parental and children's rights/wishes (Read et al., 2006).

This is particularly the case with regard to young carers who it has been argued are deprived of their childhoods, fearful, isolated and confused; experience problems with attendance, relationships and exclusion; can

(Continued)

(Continued)

have restricted psychological, social and physical development; experience impairments, injuries and educational underperformance; and can be punished for non-attendance, forced into care proceedings and overall be denied the experience of childhood (Aldridge and Becker, 1995).

The difficulties of integrated approaches to disability have been identified in service approaches to disabled adults (Wates, 2003). In particular, disabled parents have reported that young carers are forced into carer roles because of the set-up of systems of funding and they have argued that more co-ordination is required between adult and children's services in the form of joint assessment (Wates, 2003). Many disabled adults have voiced concerns that there has been too much of a shift to focusing on supporting children and not adults; a tendency to blame disabled parents; an expansion of child carer services that do not connect with adult services; time lost to disputes over prevalence rather than finding joint solutions; and little research on the effectiveness of young carers' services (Newman, 2002). A number of authors have been heavily critical of the tendency for service providers to focus in a deficit way on parental impairment at the expense of understanding the effects that more social issues such as poverty, parenting style, marital discord and social disadvantage have on children (Newman, 2002; Stables and Smith, 1999).

Much writing on young carers has overlooked children's capacities to resist and recover from adversity (Newman, 2002). Young carers themselves have highlighted how service providers have ignored their views and met with disbelief the suggestion that their lives can be rewarding (Stables and Smith, 1999). It is argued that they see themselves as children not victims (Stables and Smith, 1999). Yet, in a similar manner to disabled children, the tendency is for their 'vicitim' status to be highlighted as a way of ensuring they attract scarce resources. Ironically, it is often the case that underlying problems with service provision go ignored within such discourses (Stables and Smith, 1999).

The literature on young carers has critiqued individualised children's rights approaches because they fail to acknowledge that families as social entities are not easily reduced to human rights discourses concerning the individual (Newman, 2002). This work contrasts with the writing of those who believe that the law can be used as a tool to force local authorities to meet children's aspirations (Read et al., 2006). It is argued that the role of human rights legislation is to mediate between the individual and the state and not within families. Here, rights are perceived to be part of the justice of strangers not kin folk (Newman, 2002). This work suggests that young carers, like all children, have a web of relationships, strong emotional ties and conflicting aspirations (Newman, 2002). Such perspectives can be linked to writers in Chapter 2 who argued that professionals in children and family services should aim to develop flexible approaches (underpinned by a notion of minimum intervention) that

(Continued)

(Continued)

consider the strengths of families/communities, attend to issues of rights/ equity and utilise informal support networks (Dolan, 2006, 2008). These approaches highlight the need for services to engage with rights based, anti-discrimination and social justice perspectives but they do so whilst highlighting the need to value all the actors who can support the child (e.g. peer group, family, community and professionals).

Conclusion

This chapter has discussed how disabled children can be involved in service development. It examined the findings from the Communications project, including the perspective that to be included disabled children require physical and emotional resources; to be listened to they require adults to understand different methods of communication; to enable change in their life circumstances they require policy makers to improve access to public transport, provide greater opportunities to experience transition to work, and offer greater access to education, leisure, play and sport. The project was partially successful in its specific aim of building relationships between service providers and disabled young people. However, the project encountered problems reaching the most senior of officials, in substantially altering the power relation between disabled children and service managers and in effecting speedy change. In particular, the young people showed some frustration at the slowness of change. It was concluded that the difficulties of achieving participation in relation to disabled children and local authority services owed much to the entrenchment of disablist attitudes. It was argued that such attitudes have been challenged by legislation, policy and guidance but that a contradiction had emerged between rights based discourses and the notion that families and communities should be put at the centre of strengths based approaches.

It is possible to conclude that whilst policies based on individual rights are useful because they act as signposts for standards we should all follow, they tend to reflect outdated 'needs' based ideas of service provision. A strengths based approach requires service providers to move away from ideas concerning impairment needs – to consider how provision can address the social issues of disability such as poverty, appropriate housing, access to transport, the ability to build relationships and opportunities for employment that also impact on adult lives.

7

Analysing Participation in Local Authorities: A Politically Nuanced Holistic Approach

This chapter includes a summary of reports written for Investing in Children and is included with the kind permission of Liam Cairns.

Chapter Overview

This case study draws from two evaluations carried out on behalf of Investing in Children (IiC) in 2007. IiC is a children's rights organisation in England which runs a membership scheme for children's services who work in participatory ways. It carries out specific projects/events, enables participatory processes and develops participation strategies with children/young people in local authority areas. This chapter discusses how this organisation enabled children and young people to be involved in local decision-making in a range of local services (e.g. schools, libraries, youth, community and other local authority providers). The chapter is separated into a number of sections that discuss the key questions that were investigated; the types of people who participated in the evaluation; the views of children and young people; the perspectives of individuals within partner agencies; and the experiences of workers and managers in membership organisations. The chapter enables readers to consider approaches for developing participatory services and how to make connections between schools and communities. It encourage readers to develop confident strategies for ensuring that planning, development and evaluation include a range of stakeholders' views.

(Continued)

(Continued)

It is concluded that it is possible for children's services to develop participatory process that enable a diverse range of children and young people to influence service development, with the following conditions:

- Services are required to develop coherent, integrated, planned, strategic, structured and sustainable approaches to participation that consistently enable processes of dialogue between adults, children and young people.

- Such approaches need to be evaluated from the perspective that different partners will employ contrasting and complementary criteria to analyse effective participation (e.g. consumerist, inclusive, developmental, political and/or protective criteria).

- It is important that any such development balances out the need for both informal and formal approaches to participation, builds on knowledge architecture, and culminates in outcomes that make local services more flexible and responsive to the needs of a wider range of children, parents and young people.

Key Questions

The evaluation was designed to investigate a number of key questions. These included:

- Did IiC enable a diverse range of children and young people to be engaged in participatory processes and respond to issues of inclusion and diversity?

- Did IiC contribute to the transformation of the status of children and young people within society, from dependents to citizens?

- Did IiC enable children and young people to transform their life experiences, put forward their own agenda and change the services they encounter?

- Did IiC meet its aspiration to enable stakeholder organisations (members and partner agencies) to achieve their aims?

- How effective were IiC's relationships with different organisations?

- Did IiC practice what they preached and achieve their aims as a human rights organisation?

- What were the barriers to effective practice and how effective were IiC at over-coming these barriers?

- How coherent, sustainable and structured was IiC's approach?

- How clear was IiC's vision and was their vision supported by senior and strategic managers?

- Did children and young people perceive IiC and its staff to be supportive?

- What criteria did different individuals employ to evaluate IiC?

The research methods employed to examine these questions included conversations, interviews, focus groups (with key stakeholders) and analysis of Investing in Children reports.

Evaluating Children and Young People's Experiences of Participation

It was immediately clear that children and young people had an extremely positive view of IiC. All of the young people praised the IiC staff for the respectful and professional approach they adopted with children and young people:

> The IiC workers are amazing, they are not discriminating at all, they treat people with equal rights and really like listen to you and they are more kind of sit back let you have your say and kind of not push in and don't have a lot of adults there – 'cause adults push in. And it learns you how to stand up for yourself and for the future.

They indicated that IiC was one of the few organisations that enabled their voices to be heard and stated that they particularly valued participating in IiC projects that enabled them to raise issues of fairness in their communities:

> We went to the counsel and actually said we are sick of people not getting equal rights and it isn't fair. We were looking at the way the police treat young uns on the streets. Like, we're stopped everywhere we go just 'cause of where we're from and 'cause were young uns. So we spoke to police officers and gave them examples of what we needed to stop us wandering the streets.

> We had to go to different places taking the joint area review group round. We took them to the main trouble spots. At our shops there was like, they have a machine to make a noise like a buzzer to get young uns away (known locally as a mosquito device) and like we wanted that changed and like some shops don't allow under 16s in after five o' clock.

They particularly enjoyed contributing to processes of change in collaboration with various agencies:

> We wrote a report, then made a DVD about what we needed for sport and leisure. It sort of sticks in people's minds if it's a DVD – we told them we didn't have enough money to go places and that many parents wouldn't let them young uns be trusted to go places.

> Transport was a specific thing to speak about because there is not much transport for disabled young people. You have to wait a lot for an accessible bus. Why should you have to wait for an accessible bus? Someone else might have wanted to talk about crime but for me it was transport. We talked to people from the bus company and they told us that from 2009 the buses will all be low liner.

This suggested that IiC was strongly focused on children and young people's agendas and that it particularly enabled local authority, private and voluntary agencies to consider children and young people's life issues. Most children and young people felt that they initiated most aspects of the projects with which they worked and that IiC's approach was remarkably different to approaches that traditionally tended to ignore their voices (e.g. those in some local schools).

Working With Diverse Groups

There was substantial evidence of IiC working on diversity issues, particularly with minority ethnic, disabled and traveller children/young people:

> I like it when the worker comes to our site, we get to do posters about what we want to change and we have now got the portacabin where we can play with play dough and the computer.

The young people were involved in a range of projects and participatory processes (some specific to them, others inclusive of all children). There was evidence that by involving diverse children in inclusive projects IiC were supporting all children and young people's learning regarding diversity issues – for example, the children/young people in a 'transport group' were particularly disability aware and had developed an understanding of how transport issues affected a range of children and young people:

> I think IiC are more aware of disability issues ... we had a lad with bad hearing on our project and they sorted out a loop. We got jaws and supernova fitted into the computer and we have also got information and newsletters in Braille.

There were many cases where young people adapted their knowledge gained in one setting to be more considerate of people in another setting. For example, one young man who had participated in a project alongside disabled young people extended his disability awareness to make suggestions concerning how participatory approaches could also be applied to Old People's Homes (where his grandmother was cared for).

Some writers differentiate between different levels of participation (e.g. listening, supporting expression, taking account of, direct involvement and power sharing) (Shier, 2001). The early stages of the continuum of participatory practice involve listening. The latter approaches involve children and young people, for example co-managing and instigating processes. This involves a shift in perspective where children and young people plan, develop and make decisions, either through collaborative partnerships with adults or with adults acting as facilitators (Davis and Hogan, 2004).

Activity

Consider for a moment the extent to which you personally have been involved in participatory approaches. For example, in your own childhood were you enabled to change things about your schooling, local leisure facilities or bus timetables? Now think about the places you have worked (you could return to your notes from the previous chapter's activities). At what level does children's participation operate in those workplaces? At a minimum did you consider children's views during your daily routines? Did you stop and listen if a child asked you something? Did you have structures for participation? Were they linked to integrated working in your local area? Could issues raised by children and young people be taken up by partner agencies? To what extent did participatory processes involve a shift in power or lead to a change in outcomes?

Children have a great deal of enthusiasm for processes of participation (Alderson, 2002). How good are you at connecting with this enthusiasm? It is important that you plan processes of participation because you believe in them and not because the idea is in vogue, as some authors suggest that tokenistic approaches to participation can do more harm than good (Katz, 1995).

Limitations of the Approach

The children and young people in the IiC study were very aware of the limitations of participatory approaches. There was some self-criticism concerning the effectiveness of their own roles in projects:

> Like with our project it wasn't as popular as we had hoped because we only put the posters up three days before – we should have spent longer doing that.

Children and young people particularly raised concerns in relation to the ability of local government to respond quickly to their issues and with regard to how effective certain projects had been:

> We got the bus now – that was probably the best bit of it all and like the street wardens, them walk round and say, 'what's going on'. They talk to you and they're canny like. We built jumps in the local shops and they let you do it as long as the shops are not open and we pick 'ur rubbish up. So like we did get some things but

some other things never change ... Like when our bus was supposed to happen last April and it's only just happened now.

I've learnt it takes time for changes so you cannot just click your fingers. It's mostly the council and not IiC that takes the time. Most of the decisions have to be made with the council committees and that's why it takes time.

Some of the councillors, like most people, were really good but sometimes it's people in suits who seem frightened of change if it's not their idea. It's much better when it's the IiC worker, they listen to us and let us organise it for ourselves.

There was a great deal of criticism of the capacity of local government and health services to respond to the issues of children and young people. Some children and young people felt that service managers acted in a way that suggested that they felt threatened by new ideas. The strongest criticism came from the nature of meetings, particularly those that were not child-friendly, where people in suits dominated discussions and dismissed the ideas of children and young people:

It can be a bit boring speaking to the council service people like. We used to go to them but it was all people in suits and nothing got done. So now we meet them here and it's much better. A person from the young people's group has like been the main person and taken charge – so we've got our agenda and we read that out then, then we'll see what can be done. Sometimes we will come to an agreement with them and other times we won't.

A number of young people were frustrated at the slow rate of change, particularly in relation to the effects that poverty had on some young people's lives:

At one of the agenda days there was a young lad who kept getting their electricity switched off and we were like something should be done about that but am not sure anything could be done. Sometimes we want to change things that come up in projects but the person in the council whose job it is to change it isn't interested.

Others were very cynical about why they were being asked to participate. For example, one local authority area involved children and young people in decisions about budgets that had involved them voting on funding for specific local projects. Whilst this approach in the main was welcomed by young people, a few pointed out that it enabled the council to avoid funding all their proposals and made the children and young people share responsibility for the need to ration funding in their local area. These comments suggested that some children and young people had very complex and considered approaches and that they wished to be able to more effectively direct local funding. Davis (2007) indicates that it should not be assumed that such children would be selfish in their attitudes to the local use of resources.

An interesting finding from the IiC study was that children and young people's criteria on how to evaluate participation were not always the same as professional perspectives and that different children and young people had different views on what constituted a good project. For example, some stressed the importance of being able to do things with friends, while others suggested IiC enabled them to meet new people. For the most part they had individual and collective reasons for joining IiC projects. Many adults have argued that participation projects should not simply be evaluated on the basis of 'outcomes' but should also be judged on the learning that they enable (Davis, 2007). There is no doubt that children and young people highly valued IiC's work because the processes of participation showed them respect and enabled them to speak out about their life issues. However, they also wished to see quicker outcomes to projects. It was concluded that both process and outcomes are important to children and young people that are involved in local authority decision-making.

An overall question emerged regarding how children and young people can be supported to ensure that the messages and learning from participatory projects have maximum impact and that learning from participatory processes can be more quickly brought together to influence a range of policy areas in an integrated way. The general aim of IiC to enable children and young people to work with agencies was successful, for example there was evidence of good local collaboration with community groups, education, police, libraries, early years providers and youth initiatives. However, this work was very reliant on specific staff in each service.

It was concluded that more work was required with partner agencies to develop strategies and processes for speeding up the timeline between children and young people's views being collected and change taking place. It was also concluded that IiC and their partners would have to consider the power relations within such processes and the extent to which children and young people could actively be involved in managing such change. That is, children and young people were found to greatly value processes that enabled them to develop their own approaches and to manage their own projects. They appreciated being involved face-to-face with service providers who took their views seriously and they aspired to be more involved in processes of service evaluation. This suggests, in keeping with Chapter 2, that children and young people show great appreciation for new structures of change within local authority integrated children's services that create spaces of dialogue, enable different 'partners' to gain experience of joint decision-making, and allow in-depth discussion of which approaches work and which do not.

The young people in this study also connected life issues such as the effects of poverty (e.g. getting your electricity turned off) with issues concerning local leisure facilities. Davis (2007) found that children and young people:

view social exclusion as stemming from the interaction of a range of issues including lack of money, lack of local facilities (e.g. transport), lack of trust/respect, lack of access to participatory processes and a lack of opportunity to access employment. At the centre of this analysis is the idea that social exclusion occurs when one of these issues prevents them from establishing or maintaining relationships with others. (Davis, 2007: 141)

This book promotes the idea of building close relationships in communities through processes of participation. However, it is important that participation is properly evaluated, challenged and questioned. The staff at IiC do not assume that participatory processes automatically work. IiC have a membership scheme that requires partner organisations to be evaluated on an annual basis. This is important because many writers have suggested that too many participatory processes lead to a very limited number of outcomes (Cairns, 2001).

Activity

Consider the limitations of the participatory approaches in this and the previous chapter. Do you have processes in your local area that enable integrated solutions to be worked through with children, parents and communities? In Chapter 2 it was suggested that calls for integrated working may simply be a smokescreen for government reluctance to deal with big structural issues (e.g. poverty). A similar complaint has been made of participation. How do you ensure that participatory processes in the places you work go beyond tokenism? How do you ensure that participation leads to change? Are there approaches that go beyond the notion of 'participatory projects', coherently address the interconnection of issues of exclusion and embed systems of dialogue, listening and change in integrated children's services?

Developing a Sustained Approach: Perspectives of Member Organisations and Partner Agencies

IiC was found to have a strong commitment to member organisations and was successful at enabling member organisations to develop participatory practices. There was evidence of strong support for and good working relationships with a range of membership organisations:

The IiC worker made us be very much more up front in what we would like to do. He made us take a step back and think more about asking children in an organised way. Eventually the young people actually helped us apply for funding. We would not have had the confidence to do that before. We did an activity programme with young people, it was more than just consultation, they got what they asked for. For example, more ICT, plasma screens, msn. They didn't get everything but they told us they would like a reason why we didn't have things and that made us much more considered about what we could offer and how we worked with them.

What was good about Investing in Children was that they valued our organisation – we tend to get missed when there is training or opportunities about children and young people because we are not a youth organisation but IiC helped us to kind of circumvent that and work together better with the council. The important thing is to understand the children and young people that use our service and improve things in an everyday sense.

This example demonstrated the transformative nature of IiC. IiC was extremely successful at enabling membership organisations to reconsider their perspectives of children and to adopt more child-centred approaches. Sometimes this involved radical change to a situation where children and young people developed their own services:

Investing in Children is like the districts' participation strategy, they signed up to it with the other services ... we will do anything in our power to support children and young people to be active citizens in their own right ... When we did the Youth Club it worked because young people were involved every step of the way and when the adults raised the problem of a charge to get in the solution was suggested by the young people. They wanted it run by adults but the young people weren't for that and they organised it themselves, designed the posters, proper security like for a club, at every stage it worked and they had a hundred young people coming regularly.

Many individuals from member organisations highlighted the long-term change in thinking that membership of IiC had brought to their staff. For example:

Sometimes youth work can be airy fairy but not this. It's caused a real change in the thinking of adults, for example, we used to have security posters up as a warning to young people who use our service. We are gradually taking down the posters and having conversation with young people who don't use our service appropriately. We know now that we don't have to react so harshly and that if there are issues we involve children in the process of managing that. It's still early days – frontline staff find some children and young people very difficult, so it is gradual but the confidence that staff have developed from working with IiC is tremendous. We started with one small piece of work and now it goes into all our organisation.

A number of participants in the evaluation process commented on the inclusive nature of IiC. It is clear that practice models have developed (agenda days, research, membership, etc.) that are accessible to children and young people from different backgrounds, and with different skills and abilities:

The youngsters in the school set up the group to look at how they could improve their area and worked with the police, the local council ... I used to run the school council and it was a bit like my agenda, my meeting and my issues but after working with IiC the youngsters took that over and it's become self governing. It's given them a real voice into the way things are run, it now offers a degree of distance and enables them to decide more of what's possible in the school.

You could talk about OFSTED but my feeling is they couldn't care less about this if you didn't hit your other targets. We don't do this because of OFSTED we do it because it really works for the youngsters. Our youngsters come from deprived backgrounds and this helps build the idea that their views matter and they can change their own lives in their area. That feeds into the Every Child Matters (ECM) agenda of keeping them safer and healthier and helps them to understand their own and other youngsters' needs, but the rationale comes from the need to relate to them and to enable them to participate because it's a good thing to do and because it helps us to plan and develop the school.

These respondents combined a range of issues when outlining the benefits of their involvement with IiC. They suggested that IiC was successful because it enabled children and young people to feel their views were being taken seriously; it allowed adults to plan better; it delivered better local services; and developed children/young people's confidence. Within this context, a number of respondents indicated that IiC had enabled them to improve the way they work with disabled children:

One of the young people working with us has extremely challenging behaviour – and the way we were supported by IiC was really encouraging. They also sorted the taxis for a young person who was a wheelchair user to attend – they oiled the wheels if you know what I mean.

The different groups got together and looked at developing a website and I felt it was a very diverse group, there were young people with disabilities, young Asian women, young men, the young women's group. Everyone was from different backgrounds and we were all working together and getting on together.

A number of respondents praised IiC for the thoughtful way it approached membership organisations:

Membership is an incredibly important part of the participation strategy. It works because it's an effective way of establishing and recognising genuine dialogue. Organisations value it. It's positive and motivational and celebrates good practice rather than haranguing about bad practice.

IiC managers are crucial to the organisation, they have a calm and effective way of building relationships with enough people so eventually it moves slower then gradually moves faster.

This finding suggested that IiC was not only an extremely inclusive organisation but that its staff also provided an extremely supportive environment. Many partner agencies were quick to praise the work of IiC, particularly around participatory budgeting:

The knowledge of investing in children and their managers has helped us to develop the concept of participatory budgeting and we are starting to see children and young people coming together around Every Child Matters agenda to put in bids for projects on social inclusion, being safe, having voice, being healthy, etc. We ran a big event where we received 25 applications and children and young people voted and chose the things to be funded and the theme that is now emerging is, 'look what happens when you trust us'. It was really interesting as projects around homeless and disabilities came in the top 5 and it makes you realise that children and young people are very discerning and not just in it for themselves. They also become aware of the limitations of local funding and the need to make sensible decisions. We have seen a knock-on effect in other organisations, for example younger children being involved in equipment for nurseries. It's not totally refined yet and we are still sometimes thinking in different ways from children and young people. We need to keep working at it.

There were some tensions between the participatory children's rights perspective of investing in children and some of their partner organisations and agencies. For example, some respondents highlighted a difference between organisations, services/agencies and individuals who were interested in setting up formal structures within which participation might occur (e.g. youth fora or school councils) and those who saw children and young people's own agenda as their first point of reference for the development of participatory processes:

Someone said the obvious place to sustain the IiC approach is in your schools with school councils. The group said this won't work in our school because the school council is formal and this work is about what we want to discuss and we have a laugh.

Rather than youth parliaments. We should have the time to design things with children and young people around how they want to contribute, an engagement strategy based on their ideas not our ideas.

Like when I was at school I was intimidated by the school council and it was good that I could do something out of school because it was more about local issues, connections, sports, leisure, youth clubs, etc.

Some respondents highlighted the need to critically reflect on processes that involve one child/young person representing a local area or class and to develop flexible approaches. Others believed that such flexible approaches would be problematic if they simply assumed that one children and young people's group that had developed to meet a specific agenda could be parachuted into another more formal structure:

There is a real problem if one of the youth workers sets up a local forum from an existing structure and thinks I am sorted because I have 'my' group. That's not negotiating with staff or the young people. That's assuming that the group want to be a part of your formal structure.

This discussion mirrors debates within the academic field of childhood studies concerning the nature and benefits of participation. Rather than perceiving this debate as a threat to IiC, many respondents stressed the view that this tension created an opportunity for IiC to enter into constructive dialogue with its various stakeholders (in keeping with Anning et al. [2006] in Chapter 2). A number of respondents suggested that IiC had already been successfully involved in balancing the needs of partner agencies and membership organisations with the agenda of children and young people. Many respondents suggested that IiC had helped the participation agenda to move on in their local area and that there was now an opportunity to refocus the participation agenda to be much more about children and young people's issues rather than the needs of individual organisations:

> It, as an organisation, is not about presenting things as a fight, it's good at creating dialogue and is reasonably good at taking a step back when it's needed – IiC's approach doesn't always go down well with traditional youth work but then traditional youth work has had to recognise the benefits of IiC because of its success in engaging with children and young people.

> The vision is not IiC or youth work or the local authority's vision – it's owned by children and young people, what they have said has to happen – so it's a mainstream voice. In order for us to keep children and young people's issues in the mainstream we need to make sure that people like the local policy team, housing and regeneration are round the table to discuss the issues that really matter to children and young people. We are pretty good in children's services but what about the big directorates? Have they changed what they do? We need to be able to work out ways for these agencies to respond quicker to children and young people's issues. We need to have an annual cycle of responding to the issues and then evaluating what we have done and the spending value.

These responses demonstrated the mature position that IiC had developed and its ability to act as a fulcrum for development of participation approaches.

Discussion: Integrated Participation Processes – Going Beyond Mere Projects

A great deal of effort has gone into analysing participative processes that have been fostered by children's organisations and that have included children's organisations working in partnership with local and national government (Tisdall and Davis, 2004). Indeed, much has been made of the need for governmental and non-governmental organisations to develop participation strategies (Cutler and Frost, 2002; Cutler and Taylor, 2003). A number of writers have questioned the role of children's organisations and whether they work for, on, or with children (Borland et al., 2001). Others argue that within the one organisation there can be many different approaches to participation, for example through membership of governing bodies, management committees, advisory boards, steering groups, forums, conferences, research projects and news groups (see e.g. Badham, 2000; Gabriel, 1998).

(Continued)

(Continued)

Defining Participation and its Benefits

The word participation covers a variety of approaches that enable children and young people to be included in organisational decision-making processes concerning a range of issues such as:

- *Finance* (fundraising, allocation of resources, budgeting)
- *Management and Human Resources* (re-writing job descriptions, recruitment, setting up school councils, running after-school clubs, designing young children's clubs, selecting staff, conducting quality audits, altering ways in which reviews are conducted, working as advocates, setting up newspapers and recruiting other children)
- *Policy Making and Decision Making* (e.g. forums, draft plans and committees)
- *Communication, Planning and Publicity* (planning openings, publications, presentations, videos, websites, conferences, residential weekends, campaigns and editing written material)
- *Processes of Defining Participation* (detailing inclusion, reflecting in groups, advising policy makers, designing training packs and discussing disclosure issues)
- *Research* (local information gathering and peer research) (see e.g. Badham, 2000; Gabriel, 1998; TCS, 2000).

Some writers suggest there are a range of benefits that children gain from experiencing participation. These can broadly be broken down into those that aid the child or society in the present (e.g. that foster the child's ability to influence their present circumstances) and those that aid the child/adult of the future (e.g. that protect the child from future dangers such as unemployment, social isolation/exclusion and poor health). More specifically these can be separated into several theoretical positions concerning the benefits of participation (see, for examples: Hogan, 2003; Kirby and Bryson, 2002; Kirby et al., 2003; Sinclair and Franklin, 2000) Davis (2009) drew from a range of sources to argue there were five benefits of participation. This chapter demonstrates a sixth benefit (I have added here the concept of inclusive benefits):

- That participation has pedagogical and developmental benefits (children can learn educationally, morally and personally from the experience)
- That participation has potential political benefits (children can change social policy, exercise rights and share power with adults)
- That participation has epistemological benefits (dialogue with children can produce improved understandings and better knowledge for academics and policy makers concerning their life conditions)
- That participation has consumer benefits (it has the potential to produce services that are better value for money, better planned and better staffed)

(Continued)

(Continued)

- That participation can make children's worlds safer and provide benefits in terms of protection (the experience of developing respectful dialogue with adults and other children will promote child protection and help to prevent child abuse)
- That participation has inclusive benefits (it has the potential to foster better relations in communities and to develop a more integrated society).

These perspectives are not mutually exclusive and are often combined within the one project. However, there can be tensions between some of these perspectives, for example consumer approaches to participation (e.g. where children's organisations, local authorities, schools and governments seek input from users to improve their organisation) and self-advocacy approaches (e.g. where organisations enable groups to raise issues for themselves) (Davis, 2007; Gabriel, 1998).

Critiques of Participation

Many authors are critical of formal attempts at civic engagement with children because they are tokenistic (Alderson, 2000, 2002; Cockburn, 1998, 2002; Moss and Petrie, 2002). This tokenism is linked to the view that adult political processes are not based on equality of access to political power and that certain groups have more access to the ear of the powerful than others (Tisdall and Davis, 2004). Attempts to create institutions to promote children's rights have not been universally successful; for example, youth parliaments are not always representative of local populations and school councils have rarely led to 'democratic communities' (Alderson, 2002; Hogan, 2003; Kirby and Bryson, 2002). The evaluation concluded that IiC enabled children and young people to access political processes of change and alter issues within their local communities. It also concluded that IiC was built on sustainable structures, underpinned by a coherent approach and embedded within wider local authority processes.

Cairns (2006) is very critical of children's participation in school councils, local government forums and youth parliaments. He makes a distinction between participation based on representational democracy and participation based on participative democracy. Cairns (2006) argues that when representative democracy is applied to children it is flawed because it often leads to children behaving like mini adults; forums that are dominated by the most resourceful children in a local area; and the agenda for debates being set by adults. He suggests, in keeping with other writers, that very often children don't know who their representative is on a local forum and that there is little evidence that such forums stimulate long-term changes in the life conditions of children (Alderson, 2002; Davis and Hogan, 2004; Hogan, 2003). Some writers argue that tokenism can be avoided by organisations adopting approaches that involve children at the earliest stages of planning, enabling projects to develop incrementally, and

(Continued)

(Continued)

allowing staff to draw on learning from previous projects that are underpinned by consistent staff support (Badham, 2000). Similarly, children who take part in participatory projects often seek resolution to issues of exclusion relating to fairness, social spaces, relationships and the exercise of life choices. Yet they also value being paid to do a job within a participatory project or having the opportunity to learn new things (Davis, 2007; Davis and Hogan, 2004). That is, children tend to hold complex notions of inclusion and participation. Some authors argue that there are different cultures of participation and organisations need to be clear about their reasons for undertaking and planning participation (Kirby et al., 2003). A number of other writers have suggested that in order to avoid technical rational approaches to participation, we need to enable discursive spaces where children and adults work through what participation and inclusion mean in local contexts (Cockburn, 2002; Moss and Petrie, 2002). The evaluation concluded that IiC was underpinned by both formal and flexible approaches to participation; that children and young people valued the process as well as the outcomes of participation; and that children and young people were enabled to be involved in sustained processes of dialogue with different agencies and organisations.

Integrated Participation: Going Beyond Participation as a Project

Most children's organisations are characterised by a tension between autonomy and self-realisation where strategic managers, operational managers and frontline staff negotiate complex power relationships. This chapter has highlighted the connection between discussions concerning formal and informal structures of participation and the view of children and young people that IiC's approach is different. In so doing, it aims to warn against tick-box approaches to participation. For example, there is a danger that local staff may resist rigid performance structures that aim to promote participation. This may be especially the case for those staff who believe in sensitive approaches to participation that try to enable individuals and organisations to grow incrementally.

It is important that new structures do not alienate staff, children, young people and parents (because children do not grow up in a void). For example, some writers have argued that there is a need for a clear direction to be provided by senior managers within children's organisations/ services (Percy-Smith et al., 2001). Yet they have also recognised that clear leadership should not be characterised by the development of rigid rules and that change needs to involve both senior management and the grassroots (Kirby et al., 2003). Percy-Smith et al. (2001) advocated a constant cycle of learning and renewal for participatory organisations. In contrast, Hyland (1997) suggested that periods of change should be followed by

(Continued)

(Continued)

periods that enabled innovation to be embedded and new practice to be consolidated. This suggests that any participatory planning in integrated services should consider the speed at which innovation occurs, the swiftness with which change will become embedded, the processes by which learning will be exchanged and the ways that agreed practice will be reinforced by a range of stakeholders. At the centre of this deliberation should be the issue of how much time and funding is available for staff and children to collaborate and learn from what has been achieved so far, and build new approaches that take account of this learning.

The question this chapter poses those working in integrated children's services and their partners is: how do we harness people's capacity to develop participatory approaches in organisational terms and maximize the potential of people and communities to contribute to the development of their local services? How do we create an organisational structure, a knowledge architecture, that has at its heart notions of participation? How do we promote participation without it becoming another oppressive performance indicator that is used to judge or injure people?

It is not enough to celebrate the uniqueness of organisations such as IiC. As we go forward, opportunities exist to take that uniqueness and shape and capitalise upon it by creating spaces in children's services – a learning environment (a learning organisation) that supports collaboration between integrated services (Moss and Petrie, 2002).

In the complex modern world we cannot assume that there is one way to unfreeze an organisation or that its nature will be similar from one day to the next. What is required is not a simplistic participation strategy but a complex knowledge architecture that enables fast and participatory dialogue with key adults and children to foster the development of quick and effective solutions (Stephen Farrier, 2007, personal communication). There is great potential for this architecture to connect the social and the technological through processes of e-development. It could be possible for organisations to develop spaces where a range of stakeholders exchange ideas. It cannot be assumed that existing organisational structures will foster learning or that tagging on ideas of participation to existing power relations within local authorities will offer effective solutions to the concerns of children and young people. Debates that consider the appropriateness of different forms of participation tend to be underpinned by contrasting ideas concerning success. That is, a project may be judged successful if it achieves specific outputs and/or outcomes (e.g. changes a local policy or improves self-esteem of participants) (Kirby et al., 2003). It may also be judged successful if it enables children and young people to experience certain processes (e.g. peer collaboration). Alternatively, it may be judged to be successful if it helps to achieve governmental objectives on anti-social behaviour. It is clear that there is no

(Continued)

(Continued)

consensus on how to judge successful participation and that individuals and organisations hold a range of competing theoretical perspectives concerning the aims of participation (Davis, 2007).

The evaluation of IiC examined how effectively the organisation operated within this wide range of approaches and considered the extent to which IiC had developed a coherent approach to participation. It is argued that children's organisations can be at the forefront of challenging systems and structures that exclude children and young people. Central to this argument is the idea that participation can only be achieved when children's organisations have a clear vision, experience leadership from strategic managers or possess participation champions at a senior level (Cutler and Taylor, 2003). The evaluation demonstrated that IiC had a clear vision and experienced the support of a range of strategic and operational managers within partner agencies and membership organisations. It also suggested that participation should not simply be the preserve of organisations but should also involve partnership with children, adults and communities (Cairns, 2006). Percy-Smith et al. (2001) suggest that the agendas of children and young people can be linked to service level agreements, information-sharing events and the development of local multi-agency protocols. But they also suggest that for this to be achieved, organisations need to put in place a coherent set of policies and principles to enable joined-up thinking and learning from participatory practice to be shared.

Conclusion

It is possible to include a diverse range of children and young people in participatory processes in integrated children's services. Such participation enables children and young people to transform their life experiences, change local services and put forward their own agenda. Children and young people prefer to be involved in processes of participation where staff are extremely supportive. A range of partners involved in participatory processes utilise contrasting and yet often complementary criteria to analyse their effectiveness (e.g. consumerist, inclusive, developmental, political and/or protective criteria). Because partners have such diverse perspectives, sustained strategic approaches are required that consistently promote processes of dialogue between adults, children and young people and enable collective consideration of the effectiveness of integrated provision. These need to be supported by integrated planning that enables a more coherent, sustainable and structured approach to

(Continued)

(Continued)

participation. It is important that any such development balances out the need for both informal and formal approaches to participation; builds on existing local knowledge-sharing networks and learning architecture; broadens the range of organisations and professionals that collaborate with each other; moves beyond local vested interests; is underpinned by contemporary understandings of organisational development; examines management hierarchies and rigid rules; investigates the utility of decentralised structures; and culminates in outcomes that make local services more flexible and responsive to the needs of a wider range of children, parents and young people.

8

Conceptual Integration in Children's Services

Chapter Overview

Chapter 2 suggested that a move to fully integrated services required professionals to shift from deficit model approaches and develop conceptual integration. It argued that conceptual integration required a strengths based approach concerned with issues of timing, choice, participation and anti-discrimination. It indicated that a range of writers had contended that professionals should move away from notions of labelling (e.g. deficit models that only see families as problems) to employ approaches that put people's own solutions at the centre of service provision. It was also argued that professionals should develop a clear philosophy to underpin their professional practice in integrated strengths based children's services. This chapter considers the arguments from Chapter 2 in relation to the conceptual issues that arise from each of the case studies. This includes a discussion of the concept of social pedagogy (related to the discussion in Chapter 3); the concept of social justice and community practice (related to the discussion in Chapter 4); deficit approaches that label children (related to the discussion in Chapter 5); the social model of disability (related to the discussion in Chapter 6); and theories of childhood diversity (related to the discussion in Chapter 7).

The activities in this chapter will enable practitioners to consider how their ideas concerning children and families relate to various concepts that underlie integrated children's services. In this chapter you will be asked to consider how your own ideas about children and families relate to both professional and personal concepts concerning, play, socialisation, agency, inclusion, family support and the politics of welfare. The main aim of this discussion will be to provide the conceptual basis for

(Continued)

(Continued)

strengths based approaches to integrated working. The chapter will encourage professionals to avoiding blaming approaches and develop complex approaches to the involvement of parents and children in service development.

This chapter will encourage practitioners to see themselves as not only people who can make a difference but also as practitioners who can analyse a range of concepts. It will summarise the concepts that enable effective practice in integrated children's services; encourage practitioners to avoid dogmatic approaches; and conclude that, by comparing different case studies of integrated working, this book has:

- followed the suggestions of Moss and Petrie (2002) and created a space for dialogue concerning the different concepts, structures and relationships that should underpin integrated working
- encouraged integrated children's service providers to reduce the social space between children, families and communities
- argued that integrated approaches require professionals to give up their vested interest and embrace the complex identities of children, parents and other professionals
- demonstrated that irrespective of the structures of integrated working, conceptual integration requires professionals to interrogate their beliefs in partnership with others and in order to enable grassroots/social justice based solutions to the problems of children, families and communities.

The Concept of Pedagogy

Chapter 3 highlighted the concept of pedagogy. Pedagogues were defined as professionals who critically analysed their practice; were adept at conflict resolution; avoided polarised debates and drew from a range of social science theories (e.g. on body, mind, attachment, socialisation, play, learning, etc.); employed creative arts/media based approaches; and worked with children/parents at 'the person' level to actively co-construct knowledge and develop strategies for change (Bruce, 2004; Cohen et al., 2004; Foley, 2008; Glenny and Roaf, 2008; Moss and Bennett, 2006; Moss and Petrie, 2002). Pedagogy was defined as an integrative concept that started with the whole child, mind, emotions, creativity, history and social identity (Cohen et al., 2004). The holistic approach of social pedagogy was related to the principles of Te Whāriki (the early childhood curriculum) that connected issues of well-being, belonging, relationships, communication, exploration, contribution, family, community, ethnicity, rights, diversity and culture (David et al., 2010; Smith et al., 2000). However, Chapter 3 also raised questions about the tendency of the concept of pedagogy to overlook issues of integrated working (e.g. in Sweden), be applied ethnocentrically and be more a way of being/practising than an actual concept. Indeed, some writing in the field of early years tends to concentrate on the child, parent and pedagogue triangle at the expense of recognising that integrated settings involve multiple relationships/perspectives, destabilising change, power relations and conceptual hierarchies/selectivity (Anning et al., 2006; Dillon et al., 2001; Fitzgerald and Kay, 2008).

It has been argued that quality services will only occur when services have a coherent basis for integrated working between professionals (Smith, 2007; Smith and Davis, 2010). Smith (2007) found in her study of family work that the move from reactive to proactive welfare approaches is not consistent or coherent. For example, Chapter 3 sought to define integrated working as encompassing a wider notion that goes beyond traditional ideas of child protection and single service delivery (Smith and Davis, 2010).

There are clear tensions between 'child protection' (focusing on investigative approaches) and the pedagogy agenda (focusing on holistic provision). Many writers have suggested that the change in philosophy, culture and practice envisaged by integrated children's services has not been achieved because of the political nature of children's services (Smith, 2007; Smith and Davis, 2010).

In relation to early years pedagogy, Tina Bruce has encouraged us to move away from polarised debates concerning theory. She demonstrated a range of theories relating to play including the ideas that play involves the construction of knowledge, enables us to build relationships, supports our bodies to develop, allows for risk/new things, and enables rehearsal of the future. Bruce (2004) contrasted these ideas with situations where adults dominate play. Thus, theory in early years is not neutral.

Activity

Consider theorists you have already read. For example, most education-based degrees (or HNCs) will discuss the writing of Piaget (1968, 1975) and Vygotsky (1978). Piaget (1968) tended to deal with children in isolation, celebrating their ability to engage with the world and Vygotsky (1978) highlighted the importance of learning by interaction with peer groups or adults. I have noticed that some students jump to conclusions and start describing the children they work with as Piagetian children and Vygotskian children. Alternatively, they blame every problem a child has on Bowlby's (1979) theory of attachment (without realising how his views now look sexist, culturally dated and foster anti-men in childcare attitudes).

(Continued)

(Continued)

This is problematic as our identities are a bit more complex than that and it reduces our identity to one single determining factor (it's deterministic). Can you think of a time/activity when you yourself have preferred to be on your own and another one where you liked to be in a group? Do both concepts have meaning in your life?

Some writers discuss different models of childhood in sociology and psychology (Corsaro, 1997). It is argued that both sociological and psychological approaches have traditionally viewed children in deterministic ways. For example, some sociologists represented the child as passive, arguing that society appropriates the child, takes it over and moulds it (Parsons and Bales, 1955). They specifically saw the child as a threat to society unless formally trained to accept society's norms (Parsons and Bales, 1955). We can see a connection between these writers and Vygotsky in the sense that adults are key to learning and/or control. Corsaro (1997) critiques these approaches because they reduce children to the state of passive objects who receive socialisation but cannot think for themselves. Dated psychological and sociological positions can be further criticised because they:

- do not take account of the influence of children's peer groups

- do not recognise differences between children who experience the same impairment, or are the same class, gender, age, religion, or ethnicity

- do not take account of children's ability to make reflective choices

- do not consider childhood across social contexts

- do not understand that children have complex identities that come out at different times in different places depending on who is present.

Such approaches have also been critiqued by contemporary psychologists for underplaying children's abilities, masking children's views, imposing totalising discourses and neglecting the rights and feelings of children (Burman, 1994, 1996; Stainton-Rogers, 2001; Woodhead and Faulkner, 2000). A number of authors suggest an alternative approach that perceives children to be innovative, creative and to not only internalise culture but also to actively contribute to shaping and changing culture (Corsaro, 1997; James and Prout, 1990; James et al., 1998).

Can you think of a child who has taught you something about the way you work – can you see that socialisation works both ways? Mayall (2000) refers to this as generational relations. She argues that the power relations can be two-way between children and adults and that both look for supportive relationships. This perspective suggests that children are not simply restrained by the structures they encounter but also shape them. In Chapter 4 we saw the importance of understanding the historical context of communities. Some post-Vygotskian writers in psychology have highlighted the need to understand the systemic, historical, cultural and social contexts within which people function in integrated children's services (see socio-cultural and activity theory) (Leadbetter et al., 2007). It is argued that we need to understand better the relationships, contradictions and tensions that exist in systems. This approach sees systems and communities as complex and dynamic.

Community and Social Justice

Chapter 4 highlighted the need for professionals to understand the socio-cultural history of the people they work with in communities. It connected strengths based approaches to the concept of community capacity building (e.g. in relation to local environments, organisations, groups/networks, self-governance, leadership and relationships) (Ball and Sones, 2004; Chaskin, 2006; Moore et al., 2005). It was concluded that cultural competence was a key part of collaborative service development and that the conceptual framework underpinning integrated working needed to be clear. It was argued that integrated service development needed to outline whether the process of integration was about planning, intervention, identity/action, relationship building, outreach and/or a way of connecting families to broader services/support systems (Chaskin, 2006). Similarly, Dolan (2006) in outlining a theory of family support identifies four types of support: concrete, emotional, advice and esteem. He also defines the 'qualities' (closeness, reciprocity and durability) and 'principles' (partnership, minimum intervention, clarity of focus, strengths based perspectives, informal networks, accessible/flexible services, self-referral, inclusion, diversity, etc.) of social support. In some ways, such discussions are similar to those concerning pedagogy that define the concept through its practice. However, Dolan (2008) also sets out a clear conceptual position that integrates ecological, social justice and social capital theories. Dealing with social justice first, Dolan (2008) draws from Honneth (2000) to define social justice as the person's right to be treated with regard/care, to be entitled to legal rights and to be recognised as having attributes and strengths. This connects rights, strengths and thoughtfulness.

Chapter 4 connected the concept of social justice to the ability of children's services to integrate community members into services through volunteering, training and employment, and the ability of children's services to develop collaborative, capacity-building, integrative and systematic approaches to working with communities. In so doing, it drew a distinction between practices that raise awareness amongst staff/parents/children and practices that actually challenge the politics and power relations of systems.

Chapter 5 related this issue to child and adolescent mental health services and contrasted social justice approaches to those that only consider an individual child's pathology and judge children against normative criteria related to developmental age and stage. Such approaches have been criticised for lacking an understanding of cultural diversity, not fully assessing the social context of children's behaviour and imposing adult ideas of what children should be (Alderson, 2000; Davis, 2006).

The concept of rights was analysed in Chapter 6 which argued that we needed to balance out individual and collective rights in processes of participation with disabled children. Davis (2006, 2007) has argued that we need to examine a range of discourses concerning children and families if we are to develop integrated, participatory and social justice solutions within children's services. Davis (2007) suggested that there have not been enough in-depth studies carried out for us to be able to claim that children's services are becoming participatory and that participation has led to better outcomes for children and families. Smith (2007) found that participation in family services was patchy but that such structures as multi-agency forums had enabled dialogue between professionals and parents (note: in the main parents are consulted but not children/young people). This led Chapter 6 to conclude that for participatory services to be effective we needed to consider the role of professionals as much as the role of parents/children. It suggested that we needed to confront labelling/deficit models of childhood that give professionals/parents an excuse to avoid examining how their own behaviour impacts on children. This chapter also indicated that there could be problems with social justice approaches if they pitted (in legal settings) members of the same family or community against each other (through accepting that children have rights in law).

Chapter 6 also discussed the concepts of empowerment, minimum intervention and rights. Many approaches to solving childhood problems involve attempts to 're-programme' children and parents through behaviour therapy, processes of peer support and approaches that force parents and children to recognise their apparently inappropriate behaviour (e.g. Webster-Stratton and Herbert, 1994). These approaches claim to 'empower' parents but seem to misunderstand the nature of 'empowerment'. That is, they are unaware of the perspective in political and disability studies that 'empowerment' is not a gift that can be provided (in a somewhat patronising way) by professionals but is a state of being which people can achieve when barriers to 'self-empowerment' are removed (such as the prejudice of teachers, social workers and other middle-class professionals) (Davis, 2006).

> ### Activity
>
> Consider your practice in relation to Chapter 4 – do you treat power as a gift? Do you believe that parents with problems need to be taught the correct way to behave or do you see them as partners, collaborators and agents? How do you build partnerships with people who have failed to care for their children? Chapter 4 encourages us to take a non-judgemental approach – is this possible?

Some studies have considered the effectiveness of parenting programmes (Hallam, 2008). They argue that contemporary group-based programmes can make limited impacts on the behaviour of children and the metal health, parenting skills and self-confidence of parents. However, many authors have critiqued these approaches because they have tended to deal with children and parents in isolation from each other (Dolan and McGrath, 2006). It has been concluded that very few of the parenting programmes (e.g. Triple P, Incredible Years and Mellow Parenting, etc.) utilised by local authorities have been properly evaluated and those that have, have tended to be evaluated by the people administering the intervention (Hallam, 2008). Parenting programmes are also believed to be problematic as they over-assume a level of readiness/order in families' lives, can lead to stigmatisation in communities, and are imported from other countries without clear evidence they are transferable (Hallam, 2008).

Contemporary approaches to families have attempted to avoid patronising parents and recognise their skills and abilities (Herbert, 2000). It is important to note here that Herbert's view shifts over time. This shift recognises the strengths of families and communities and the structural causes of inequality that lead people to experience lives characterised by stress and conflict. Davis (2006) connected such notions from childhood studies, disability studies and political studies to argue for a movement to an approach that puts children at the centre of the discussion concerning their life problems. Davis (2006) builds on the work of other authors who have moved away from structural and materialist approaches in sociology that tended to only associate childhood with ascribed identities such as class or gender and family therapy approaches that have tended to only see the child as part of a wider system and not as a social agent (Hill, 2005).

Deficit Approaches that Label Children

Chapter 5 drew from writers that have encouraged us to investigate the interconnectedness of 'the body' to social places and the importance of understanding the role of social relations in different social locations (Dyck, 1999; Stables and Smith, 1999; Valentine, 1999). It concluded that many young people highlighted the importance of the social as well as the organisational aspects of mental health services. It argued (in keeping with Chapter 2) that integrated services should confront conceptual differences because parents, teachers, counsellors, psychologists and medical professionals can fall into the trap of labelling children and young people rather than making their wishes central to building strong, supportive and trustful relationships.

Chapter 5 differentiated between deficit model approaches and those (e.g. Bronfenbrenner's [1989] ecological model) that have recognised issues outside of the individual child (perceiving the child to be at the centre of a series of rings that included their immediate friends, school and neighbours, wider structures such as school policies/local services, and issues related to national culture, government and the media). Ecological approaches are much more complex than individualised approaches and give a firm basis for family/community support (Dolan, 2008). However, it was argued there was still a tendency for some professionals who take an ecological approach to decide what the structural solutions are to children's problems and to fail to include parents and children in processes of decision-making (thus failing to make connections to ideas of social justice).

The strength of ecological approaches lies in the fact that they recognise the systems around the child and family. Such approaches have led people in the UK to argue that the problems of children and families (e.g. poverty) can be addressed by getting parents into employment or by redistributing resources through things like family credit (Davis, 2007). These perspectives have attempted to promote ways of overcoming systemic inequality. However, the weakness of these approaches centre on the fact that they generally highlight the deficits of communities and families whilst overlooking how the politics of systems within local authorities create problems for families (e.g. how vested interests, fights over scarce resources and in-fighting between services create barriers for parents and children) (Smith and Davis, 2010). That is, such approaches do not question how parents/children locally experience the 'surveillance' roles and practices of the professionals who work with them (e.g. how the young people in Chapters 5 and 7 felt about having to engage with professionals wearing suits).

More politically aware and complex approaches have been developed that attempt to shift children's services from hierarchical approaches that assume that the professional knows best to a position where service users are assumed to be the experts on their own lives and professionals are believed to be the experts at facilitating processes of resolution (Davis, 2007; Dolan, 2008). Chapter 7 connected these approaches to writing on multi-agency working that aimed to ensure that no one professional defines children's 'problems' or the solutions to their life issues. It promoted processes that enable dialogue between parents, children and service providers, earlier identification of issues and 'joined up' approaches to service provision. For example, Moss and Petrie (2002) were employed in the chapter to suggest that we need to move from thinking about children's services as a set of adult rules, norms, principles and rationales to basing children's services on contingent relationships that enable surprise, doubt and uncertainty. This shift requires professionals to balance their aspirations with those of children and young people. Moss and Petrie (2002) suggest that local authorities need to create 'discursive space' that enable adults and children to contest understandings, values, practices and knowledge and promote different ways of thinking about ethics, relationships, practices and structures. This needs to happen because in social spaces (particularly when different values remain hidden) individuals vie with each other to impose their ideas of what constitutes legitimate practice (Bourdieu, 1978).

Dolan (2008) and Dolan and McGrath (2006) have connected social justice approaches to the concept of social capital (the development of community bonds of support) (Coleman, 1998; Putnam et al., 1993). Some writers argue that social capital is a prerequisite for community regeneration (Broadhead et al., 2008; Jones and Leverett, 2008). Davis (2007) has connected social capital discourses to those concerning the social model of disability in disability studies.

In a similar way, Chapter 5 dealt with the concept of integrated mental health services and differentiated between individual, group and holistic approaches to service delivery. There has been a huge movement in counselling studies from approaches that traditionally labelled people to ones that adopt a strengths based approach. In the 1980s, Strategic Family Theory and Therapy looked at the whole family as a system/context where problems developed and were maintained. This approach in the most part attempted to change behaviour by hypothesising about deficits, reframing ways of thinking and getting people to repeat behaviours. In particular it claimed to be politically neutral and believed that professionals should not show themselves to 'patients' (Haley, 1980; Madanes, 1981; Selvini et al., 1978).

 Activity

Can you connect this approach with Chapter 5 – what did the young people say about professionals who remained neutral and kept asking them 'how do you feel'?

(Continued)

(Continued)

Chapter 3 argued (using the concept of pedagogy) that professionals should interact at 'the person' level. Yet, this chapter has concluded that the pedagogue position does not choose between different theories. Can you see how problematic this is when trying to develop strengths based and integrated approaches? This is the real difficulty with integrated services. Practitioners have to balance the need to value different perspectives on children and families with the need to also be honest about the politics of their practices. Practitioners are asked not to take sides between different theories or concepts of childhood, yet the people they work with often do. Can you think of how to balance the way theory impacts on your practice without becoming politically neutral and mundane? They key issue here is to connect the idea that all concepts of children and families have pros and cons with the argument that practitioners can rarely be neutral because they have both personal and professional prejudices which they themselves may not always be aware of. In these moments it is important for you to be clear about why you are recommending, arguing for or implementing a specific approach. Is the decision political? Does it relate to your own or other people's vested interest? Some decisions are more difficult than others (e.g. those relating to child protection) and sometimes it is not possible to make them in participatory ways. How do you make the judgement on when to make a decision, when to celebrate the power of others to make choices and when to seek/build consensus. The fluid nature of children's services means that it is important that professionals draw from a range of approaches when responding to everyday issues (hence Bruce's 2004 call for us to resist dogma). However, this does not mean that practitioners should ignore the politics of their aspirations, beliefs and practices.

Chapter 2 demonstrated that integrated teams require professionals to recognise the politics of their professional and personal perspectives and to utilise them during meetings (Anning et al., 2006). This request is similar to the major shift in counselling studies concerning power relations that started with the development of solutions based approaches that avoided defining the individual as a problem (Berg and DeJong, 1996; De Shazer and Molnar, 1987; Miller and De Shazer, 2000). Such approaches were influenced by feminist, post-structural and post-modern perspectives that considered issues of power/politics, moved away from the hierarchical approaches (that, for example, privileged the role of the medical professional/counsellor), highlighted the possibility of collaborative practice, recognised the expertise of all people and questioned notions of authority/truth (Corker and Shakespeare, 2001). This post-modern turn also occurred in disability studies.

The Social Model of Disability and its Critique

The 'traditional' 'British' Union of the Physically Impaired Against Segregation (UPIAS, 1976) social model definition of disability described disability as a phenomenon that was created by society's structures and attitudes (e.g. inaccessible buildings, negative stereotypes about disabled people's inabilities, intransigent welfare rules). This approach aimed to avoid conflating disability with illness/ impairment (Kasnitz and Shuttleworth, 1999). There are many similarities between discourses concerning social capital and those concerning disability. Indeed, in both fields service providers unreflexively impose their ideas of 'normal childhood' to create the concept of children in 'special need'. In disability studies medics, social workers, teachers, psychologists and other adults are criticised for promoting a notion of the disabled child as passive and vulnerable and as an object to be fixed (Davis et al., 2003; Priestley, 1998; Shakespeare and Watson, 1998). A number of writers have demonstrated that in everyday settings adults and children often characterise disabled children as:

- incapable of making choices

- not viewing the world as we see it

- needing structured and adult-controlled play and leisure opportunities

- a danger to themselves and the people they work with

- as unable to follow social conventions (not knowing the correct way to behave) (e.g. Davis and Watson, 2001a and b).

These perspectives have been challenged by writing that has demonstrated that not all adults and non-disabled children accept these discourses (Davis and Watson, 2001a and b; Davis et al., 2000). For example, some professionals are reflexive (question how they work with children).

Chapter 6 critiqued social model perspectives for defining disabled children as social victims. Many writers have been critical of the rigid nature of the social model and of the way it leads to a simplistic characterisation of 'disability culture' (Corker and Davis, 2001; Davis, 2000; Davis and Corker, 2001). Disability studies in the UK has been criticised for inadequately understanding difference, for ignoring disabled people who experience inequality on the basis of 'gender', 'race' and 'sexuality' (Morris, 1992; Vernon, 1997) and for conflating impairment with both disability and chronic illness (Corker, 1999b). Most recently, it has become apparent that there are many 'social models' of disability, ranging from materialist to post-modern versions (Corker, 1999a; Corker and Shakespeare, 2001). Corker and Shakespeare (2001) defined three types of post-modernism: *radical post-modernism* (which suggests there are multiple local knowledges, truth is contested and life is ambiguous); *psychoanalytical approaches* (which argue that people hold diverse fragmented notions of identity; there can be confusion/uncertainty concerning legitimate behaviour and people balance contradictory ideas in their heads on a daily basis); and *performativity* (which contends that people interpret reality through social practice, people can take on diverse/contradictory roles and identity does not simply come from genetics).

Some writers have argued that we must be wary of presenting cultural constructions as a given (Whyte, 1995). These approaches have encouraged us to question traditional ideas concerning legitimate behaviour and authority and have promoted a complex view of disability, culture and identity where disability is no longer only viewed as something that you 'are' (e.g. in terms of physical characteristics) but is recognised as something that you 'experience' in different ways, depending on who else is present (Corker and Davis, 2000, 2001). This fluid description of disability has enabled writers to examine differences within as well as between groups (Davis, 2000). It can also be connected to fluid descriptions of ethnicity that encourage us to move away from exoticising difference and to realise that young people 'do ethnicity' in different ways (Nayak, 2009). Such approaches encourage us to avoid seeing children as social victims.

Activity

Consider how contemporary approaches to play, psychology, disability studies, family/community studies, ethnicity, social justice, mental health and counselling pose questions concerning who you work with in specific professions and the concepts that underlie our practice. In particular, you need to consider why a specific intervention, process or service should be employed with specific children, families and communities. You also need to question your concept of service delivery. For example, does your service work with specific children in isolation? How do you know that this work is effective? Is it part of the role (e.g. being a teacher on his/her own in a class) or due to some other reasons (e.g. it's always been that way). Can you map out the ways you can open up your work settings and disperse power (e.g. if you are a teacher inviting in parents and other professionals). Can you consider using approaches that include diverse children (e.g. in Chapter 7 the IiC research indicated that many children had learnt a lot about societal barriers around transport because the process of developing the transport service involved disabled and non-disabled children and young people).

This raises the question, why do we offer particular services? Chapter 2 argued that we needed to balance universal, targeted, developmental, compensatory and protective services (Gilligan, 2000; Glenny and Roaf, 2008). Compensatory approaches suggest that we work with children and families because they are lacking something. When coupled with social capital theory, we might create services to compensate children/families who do not have strong social ties, have not had a successful education and have not benefited from having 'good' role models (e.g. sure starts). We might try to employ developmental community capacity-building approaches to strengthen them and their communities (e.g. adult education) (Gilligan, 2000). Alternatively we may produce protective services (e.g. support groups/workers) because we believe that unless we intervene early in children's lives and help families out of difficult situations, then children may be prevented from experiencing a full childhood or developing into successful adults.

In political studies, 'social integrationist' perspectives have connected adult success to issues of education and employment (Davis, 2007). They have suggested that we need to compensate people who have missed out on opportunities to learn and work (e.g. through additional training/job clubs, etc.). These perspectives can be contrasted with moralist perspectives that blame people's lack of opportunity on their own lack of values, get up and go and commitment (Davis, 2007; Levitas, 1998). Moralist perspectives have been strongly rejected by those who call for greater redistribution of resources to families to overcome inequality and poverty (Levitas, 1998). Chapter 3 indicated that it was interesting that the concept of integrated children's services is not present in countries such as Sweden where economic inequalities are reduced by strong welfare provisions. This book has not spent much time considering the issue of economic redistribution because the issue is mostly overlooked in the writing on integrated children's services. Indeed, social capital and integrationist ideas (which connect ideas of social cohesion, education and employment) are much more prevalent.

Activity

Chapters 3, 4 and 7 considered issues of employment and indicated that some writers connect participatory processes with the opportunity for children and young people to develop work skills. There are tensions between different forms of welfare provision.

It is important to be clear about the nature of service provision and why a specific approach is being utilised. Is it simply that there is no money?

(Continued)

(Continued)

If that is the case, what alliances can you build to make sure there are suitable alternatives? Have you explained the different types of approaches to service users and agreed the combination that best suits them?

Consider the discussion above about compensatory, development and protective services. How do you view your profession, workplace or job role? What types of services/practices do you provide? Do you do things to children/families or with them?

Consider the comments from the professionals in Chapter 7. Do you have fears about working with children and families like the professional whose service involved lots of rules that limited children's access? Who could you discuss these feelings with? Can you build relationships with local children, families and/or organisations (like the services in Chapters 5 and 7) so that you don't feel so isolated?

Theories of Childhood, Complexity and Diversity

Chapter 4 indicated the requirement for integrated services to examine differences within groups and to develop complex explanations concerning the relationship between identity, group and society. In anthropology Asad (1986) has argued that we have different cultures within apparently similar groupings. In disability studies Corker suggested: 'disabled identity is imbued with multiple and fluid meanings which reflect and create context' (Corker, 1999a: 195). In other fields (e.g. queer theory) writers such as Seidman (1998) have resisted the notion of unitary sexual identities by questioning 'the social forces that compel selves and social relations to be organised in sexual identity terms' (Seidman, 1998: 185). The suggestion is that we should be investigating uniform notions of identity, culture and structure and that this investigation should enable us to gain insight into how people respond to the individuals, structures and cultures they encounter on a daily basis. Monk and Frankenberg (1995) drew on different voices of disabled people who had written about Multiple Sclerosis to illustrate the complex ways that identity is interrelated with culture and structure. They indicated that the accounts in the various texts are similar yet different because they are shaped by 'a particular conceptualisation of the self and of the temporal processes of sickness, interwoven with a particular organisation of health care and knowledge' (Monk and Frankenberg, 1995: 130). They break down the idea of cultures as fixed and opposite.

Frankenberg's (2000) work complements the works of theorists who have contributed to our understandings of the complexity of childhood (e.g. James and Prout, 1990, 1995; James et al., 1998). He suggests that rather than completely jettisoning the concept of culture, we should investigate the relationship between cultural values and the temporality of 'real life' events (Frankenberg, 2000). This is similar to the work of other writers who have argued that by comparing cultures across or within geographical areas, we can learn about the systems that influence people's lives at the same time as representing the everyday differences of those lives (Marcus, 1986; Marcus and Fischer, 1986). Christensen (1999) has argued that most projects concerning children and health are disappointing because the way they are constructed prevent people understanding the child's perspective or engaging with children's everyday cultures. Indeed, sociological studies on health and social capital in the UK are dominated by interview and statistically based studies and over-emphasise adult perspectives on childhood, poverty and health (Christensen, 1999; Morrow, 1999). Similarly, social capital theorists have tended to sideline children's own perspectives (e.g. only examining the negative affects on their lives of adult-based problems) (Morrow, 1999).

This critique suggests that the work of social capital theorists can be just as deterministic as the outdated deficit psychological normalisation approaches (highlighted in Chapter 5); the approaches to family support that isolate the child from the parent (discussed in Chapter 4); and medical model perspectives that suggest disabled children are passive and vulnerable (see Priestley, 1998). These approaches only paint a partial picture of childhood because they fail to understand that children are a diverse group, that different children can develop their own contradictory ways of generating social capital and that they do not have a uniform way of experiencing social exclusion (Davis, 1996, 1999).

This also raises questions regarding children's own aspirations for services. Researchers have indicated that children feel excluded for a number of reasons, including 'unfair' engagement with public servants (e.g. the police or teachers), not having a home you're happy to bring a friend to, not having access to transport to visit friends, not being able to go with your friends to play/ leisure areas, not having acceptable clothing and not being able to gain access to school-related events, equipment or opportunities (Davis, 2007; Morrow, 2000; Ridge, 2002). Davis (2007) concluded that:

- Children/young people and adults that inhabit a social space have complex identities and form complex allegiances

- Different children/young people in the same setting have contrasting opportunities to form mutually respectful relationships

- Those who do not have access to respectful relationships are keenly aware of how this deficit has consequences for their inclusion

- Social inclusion relates to process as much as resources, is relative, involves agency (is caused by the acts of others) and can be dynamic (influence the present as well as the future)

- Exclusion can mean different things to the same person in different contexts

- Specific people/groups intentionally and unintentionally act to exclude others in different ways in diverse locations

- All individuals and groups are capable of exclusion and inclusion (e.g. a child bullying/being bullied)

- The socially excluded need not be characterised as homogenous groups

- Everyone has the potential to act in powerful ways and has the capacity to act in both integrative and divisive ways (Davis, 2007: 135).

Davis (2007) promotes a social dynamic approach to working with children that he suggests is useful because:

> It moves us away from patronising approaches to social inclusion that characterise specific groups as victims. It also moves away from rigid definitions of socially excluded young people that separate them out into neatly boxed groups. (Davis, 2007: 135)

This suggests that different social actors react in different ways to the same initiative and that a specific solution to integrated working will not work in the same way, in the same context on separate occasions (Davis, 2007). Many psychological and sociological accounts of child health (associated with social capital approaches) fix the child and in so doing, they demonstrate little awareness of the tension between control and self-realisation in child–adult relationships (for further discussion of this tension see Prout [2000]). These fixed accounts fail to recognise that children are active social agents, have fluid identities and can resist stereotypes about themselves (Corker and Davis, 2001; Davis and Watson, 2001b).

Some writers have been critical of the development of the concept of child 'agency' because they feel it has isolated the child from other socio-cultural influence (e.g. Toren, 2001). Most authors in childhood studies have not focused on children's agency at the expense of structural and cultural factors that influence children's lives. They focus their attention on understanding how child agency influences and is influenced by different social and cultural processes (e.g. James and Prout, 1995). Chapter 7 discussed how children and young people were involved in local decision-making in a range of local services (e.g. schools, libraries, youth and community services and those of other local authority providers).

However, Chapter 7 also critiqued the notion of participation, concluding that for it to be effective it needed to enable professionals, families, children and young people to access political processes of change, alter issues within their local communities, and build coherent, embedded and sustainable structures. Indeed, a distinction was made between participation based on representational democracy and participation based on participative democracy (Cairns, 2006). At the centre of this discussion was the realisation that service providers needed to engage with complex notions of inclusion and participation. Chapter 7 argued that children's organisations can be at the forefront of processes that challenge systems and structures that exclude children and young people and Chapter 4 encouraged us to see the strengths and complex identities of service users. Similarly, Chapter 6 argued that:

- In the complex modern world we cannot assume that there is one way to unfreeze an organisation

- Integrated children's services do not require simplistic participation strategies but a complex knowledge architecture that enables fast and participatory dialogue

- It cannot be assumed that existing organisational structures will foster such dialogue

- Individuals and organisations hold a range of competing theoretical perspectives concerning the aims of participation.

This position requires us to consider the complex nature of children, families and professionals. In particular, it demonstrates that it is just as important to break down stereotypes about professionals as it is to break down those about children because the knowledge that we gain can be utilised to stimulate policy change by promoting integrated practice. A politically nuanced holistic strengths based approach requires participation at different levels of integrated practice (face to face, local teams/forums, complex/acute provision, strategic management, area planning, etc). This can and must also involve local children, young people and adults taking control of their own solutions, building lasting partnerships and finding quicker answers to their life problems.

Conclusion

This book has attempted to compare different case studies to better understand the concepts, structures and relationships that underpin integrated children's services. This chapter has endeavoured to summarise

(Continued)

(Continued)

the key conceptual issues that could underpin a strengths based approach to integrated children's services.

The holistic concept of pedagogy was considered as a source of conceptual integrations, however despite its usefulness it was argued that it overlooked issues of integrated working (e.g. in Sweden), tended to be applied ethnocentrically and was more a way of being/practising than an actual concept. In particular, it was concluded that problems exist with conceptually neutral approaches to pedagogy because they do not leave professionals well placed to challenge deficit models, nor help practitioners engage with political dynamism, nor encourage them to take part in the sort of open and honest integrated discussion that writers called for in Chapter 2 (e.g. Anning et al., 2006).

This chapter has also discussed the concept of social justice and community practice. It was concluded that we need to balance out concepts of individual and collective rights, that power should not be used as a gift and that individualised approaches are problematic (e.g. parenting programmes). In particular, it was concluded that we need to examine a range of discourses concerning children and families if we are to develop integrated, participatory and social justice solutions within children's services. The chapter examined such discourses in the section that considered deficit approaches that label children. It was concluded that ecological models had their strengths (e.g. they looked at the child and family in a systemic way), but more politically aware and complex approaches were required that questioned hierarchy (the assumption that the professional knows best), promoted the idea that service users are the experts on their own lives and required professionals to be experts at facilitating processes of resolution (Davis, 2007; Dolan, 2008).

The concept of social capital was related to the social model of disability, however these theories were both seen as problematic. Indeed, they were critiqued for creating 'social victims' and rarely engaging with contemporary ideas concerning childhood, gender, ethnicity, etc. The section on disability concluded by contrasting such rigid theoretical perspectives with post-structural approaches that challenge traditional authority and promote the idea that identity is complex, fluid and ever changing. (It should be noted that this critique does not mean that social model and capital approaches should be totally rejected, rather, that these approaches should be used where they can be most effective, e.g. when attempting to remove structural barriers to learning or addressing inequality through redistribution

(Continued)

(Continued)

and more complex approaches should be employed when professionals are trying to quickly unblock cultural problems in organisations and/or enabling children, families and communities to resolve their life problems without structural or professional intervention.)

The final section of this chapter discussed theories of childhood complexity and diversity. It was concluded that there must be spaces for dialogue in contemporary integrated children's services because the fluid nature of the lives of children, families and professionals means that our expectations and understandings are constantly changing.

It was also concluded that such spaces of dialogue benefit from the theoretical understanding that all individuals and groups are capable of exclusion and inclusion. Such a theoretical starting point requires us to constantly question our thoughts, practices and relationships. It requires us to consider integrated services as socially dynamic spaces where solutions to people's problems can be both inclusive and exclusive. It also enables this book to conclude that in such complex social spaces, there will be numerous ways to develop flexible integrated services and that we should not assume that any one approach will work best or can be parachuted in (e.g. from another country).

The activities in this chapter asked you to consider how your own ideas about children and families related to both professional and personal concepts concerning play, socialisation, agency, inclusion, family support and the politics of welfare. The activities aimed to demonstrate that theories shift over time. I hope that this encourages you to avoid assuming that any professional has only one concept in their head at any one time. This chapter aimed to provide the conceptual basis for strengths based approaches to integrated working. It encouraged professionals to develop thoughtful approaches, concepts and relationships. A central conclusion of the book is that irrespective of the structures of integrated working, conceptual integration requires professionals to consider their conceptual starting points in relation to ideas of social justice, empowerment, minimum intervention and community capacity building. Without a politically nuanced perspective, you will not be able to build partnerships with others and enable grassroots solutions to be developed to the problems of children, families and communities.

The chapters in this book have attempted to set out a way that integrated children's services can aim to reduce the social space between children,

(Continued)

(Continued)

parents, communities and service providers by encouraging people to value difference and develop interdependencies. However, interdependency can only be generated where people are willing to give up their vested interests and power bases and enter into meaningful dialogue (Smith and Davis, 2010). I hope the book has encouraged you to reduce the social space between yourself, children, families and communities, to consider your prejudices and embrace the complex identities of children, parents and other professionals. I also hope it enables you to remember (as you develop your careers) that integrative processes can be obstructed when professionals become so hung up on their own self-importance they forget to ask the people they work with how they want to improve their life conditions.

Marcus (1986) has suggested that we can explore how different localities are interlinked by unintended consequences of actions within them and local areas are embedded in a wider system. He proposes that we analyse the contrasting and conflicting relations between individuals who inhabit a social location. I hope that this book has created the space for a variety of perspectives to be valued and, through processes of self-recognition, dialogue and change, will inspire you to work and develop integrated children's services that enable a variety of children, young people, families, communities and professionals to self-empower themselves on an everyday basis.

References

Alderson, P. (1993) *Children's Consent to Surgery.* Buckingham: Open University Press.

Alderson, P. (1995) *Listening to Children: Children, Ethics and Social Research.* Essex: Barnardo's.

Alderson, P. (2000) *Young Children's Rights: Exploring Beliefs, Principles and Practice.* London: Jessica Kingsley.

Alderson, P. (2002) 'Student rights in British schools: Trust, autonomy, connection and regulation', in R. Edwards (ed.) *Children, Home and School: Autonomy, Connection or Regulation.* London: Falmer Press.

Aldgate, J. (2006) 'Children, development and ecology', in J. Aldgate, D. Jones, W. Rose and C. Jeffrey (eds) *The Developing World of the Child.* London: Jessica Kingsley.

Aldgate, J. and Tunstill, J. (1995) *Implementing Section 17 of the Children Act.* London: HMSO.

Aldridge, J. and Becker, S. (1995) 'The rights and wrongs of children who care', in B. Franklin (ed.) *The Handbook of Children's Rights.* London: Routledge.

Aldridge, M. and Evetts, J. (2003) 'Rethinking the concept of professionalism: The case of journalism', *The British Journal of Sociology,* 54(4): 547–64.

Anning, A., Cottrell, D., Frost, N., Green, J. and Robinson, M. (2006) *Developing Multiprofessional Teamwork for Integrated Children's Services.* Maidenhead: Open University Press.

Asad, T. (1986) 'The concept of cultural translation in British social anthropology', in G. Marcus and J. Clifford (eds) *Writing Culture.* Berkeley, CA: University of California Press.

Aubrey, C. (2010) 'Leading and working in multi-agency teams', in G. Pugh and B. Duffy (eds) *Contemporary Issues in the Early Years.* London: Sage.

Avery, D. (1999) 'Talking "tragedy": Identity issues in the parental story of disability', in M. Corker and S. French (eds) *Disability Discourse.* Buckingham: Open University Press.

Badham, B. (2000) *'So Why Don't You Get Your Own House in Order?' Towards Children and Governance in The Children's Society.* London: The Children's Society.

Ball, J. and Sones, R. (2004) 'First Nations early childhood care and development programs as hubs for intersectoral service delivery', paper presented at the Second International Conference on Local and Regional Health Programmes, Quebec City, 10 October.

Banks, S. (1998a) 'Codes of ethics and ethical conduct: A view from the caring professions', *Public Money and Management,* 18(1): 27–30.

Banks, S. (1998b) 'Professional ethics in social work – what future?', *British Journal of Social Work,* 28: 213–31.

Beckett, C. (2003) 'The language of the seige: Military metaphors in the spoken language of social work', *British Journal of Social Work,* 33(5): 625–39.

Beresford, B. (1997) *Personal Accounts: Involving Disabled Children in Research.* York: Social Policy Research Unit.

Berg, I.K. and DeJong, P. (1996) 'Solution-building conversations: Co-constructing a sense of competence with clients', *Families in Society: The Journal of Contemporary Human Services,* 77: 376–91.

Bertram, T., Pascal, C., Bokhari, S., Gasper, M. and Holtermann, S. (2002) *Early Excellence Centre Pilot Programme: Second Evaluation Report 2000–2001.* Nottingham: DfES Publications.

Billingham, K. and Barnes, J. (2009) 'The role of health in early years services', in G. Pugh and B. Duffy (eds) *Contemporary Issues in the Early Years*. London: Sage.

Blackburn, C. (1994) 'In sickness and in health', in T. David (ed.) *Working Together for Children*. London: Routledge.

Borland, M., Hill, M., Laybourn, A. and Stafford, A. (2001) *Improving Consultation with Children and Young People in Relevant Aspects of Policy-Making and Legislation in Scotland*. Edinburgh: Stationary Office.

Bourdieu, P. (1978) 'Sport and social class', *Social Science Information*, 12(6): 819–40.

Bowlby, J. (1979) *The Making and Breaking of Affectional Bonds*. London: Tavistock.

Bradshaw, J. (1990) *Child Poverty and Deprivation in the UK*. London: National Children's Bureau.

Bricher, G. (2001) 'If you want to know about it just ask. Exploring disabled young people's experiences of health and health care', unpublished PhD thesis, University of South Australia.

Broadhead, P., Meleady, C. and Delgado, M.A. (2008) *Children, Families and Communities: Creating and Sustaining Integrated Services*. Maidenhead: Open University Press.

Bronfenbrenner, U. (1989) 'Ecological systems theory', in R. Vasta (eds) *Annals of Child Development, Vol. 6*. Greenwich, CT: JAI Press, pp. 187–249.

Brooker, L. (2002) *Starting School: Young Children Learning Cultures*. Buckingham: Open University Press.

Brooker, L. (2005) 'Learning to be a child: Cultural diversity in early years ideology', in N. Yelland (ed.) *Critical Issues in Early Childhood Education*. Maidenhead: Open University Press.

Brown, M. (1994) 'Voluntary agencies, young children and their families: Preschool playgroups', in T. David (ed.) *Working Together for Children*. London: Routledge.

Bruce, T. (2004) *Developing Learning in Early Childhood*. London: Sage.

Burman, E. (1994) *Deconstructing Developmental Psychology*. London: Routledge.

Burman, E. (1996) 'Local, global or globalized? Child development and international children's rights legislation', *Childhood*, 3(1): 45–66.

Cairns, L. (2001) 'Investing in children: Learning how to promote the rights of all children', *Children and Society*, 15(5): 347–60.

Cairns, L. (2006) 'Participation with purpose', in K. Tisdall, J. Davis, M. Hill and A. Prout (eds) *Children, Young People and Social Inclusion*. Bristol: Policy Press, pp. 217–34.

Chaskin, R.J. (2006) 'Family support as community-based practice: Considering a community capacity framework for family support provision', in P. Dolan, J. Canavan and J. Pinkerton (eds) *Family Support as Reflective Practice*. London: Jessica Kingsley.

Cheung, M. and Leung, P. (2006) 'Culturally appropriate family support practice: Working with Asian populations', in P. Dolan, J. Canavan and J. Pinkerton (eds) *Family Support as Reflective Practice*. London: Jessica Kingsley.

Christensen, P. (1999) 'Towards an anthropology of childhood sickness: An ethnography of Danish school children', PhD thesis, University of Hull.

Christie, D. and Menmuir, J.G. (2005) 'A common standards framework as a catalyst for inter-professional collaboration in teaching and the caring professions', *Policy Futures in Education*, 3(1): 62–74.

Clark, M. and Waller, T. (2007) 'Introduction', in M. Clark and T. Waller (eds) *Early Childhood Education and Care: Policy and Practice*. London: Sage.

Clarke, J. and Newman, J. (1997) *The Managerial State: Power, Politics and Ideology in the Remaking of Social Welfare.* London: Sage.

Cockburn, T. (1998) 'Children and citizenship in Britain', *Childhood,* 5(1): 99–118.

Cockburn, T. (2002) 'Concepts of social inclusion/exclusion and childhoods', paper presented at the ESRC Children and Social Inclusion Seminar, University of Edinburgh, December.

Cohen, B., Moss, P., Petrie, P. and Wallace, J. (2004) *A New Deal For Children? Re-Forming Education and Care in England, Scotland and Sweden.* Bristol: Policy Press.

Coleman, J. (1998) 'Social capital, human capital, and investment in youth', in A. Petersen and J. Mortimer (eds) *Youth Unemployment and Society.* Cambridge, MA: Harvard University Press.

Corker, M. (1999a) 'New disability discourse, the principle of optimization, and social change', in M. Corker and S. French (eds) *Disability Discourse.* Buckingham: Open University Press.

Corker, M. (1999b) 'Differences, conflations and foundations: The limits to the accurate theoretical representation of disabled people's experience', *Disability & Society,* 14(5): 627–42.

Corker, M. and Davis, J.M. (2000) 'Disabled children – invisible under the law', in J. Cooper and S. Vernon (eds) *Disability and the Law.* London: Jessica Kingsley.

Corker M. and Davis, J.M. (2001) 'Portrait of Callum: The disabling of a Childhood', in R. Edwards (ed.) *Children, Home and School: Autonomy, Connection or Regulation.* London: Falmer Press.

Corker, M. and Shakespeare, T. (2001) 'Mapping the terrain', in M. Corker and T. Shakespeare (eds) *Disability and Postmodernity.* London: Continuum.

Corsaro, W.A. (1997) *The Sociology of Childhood.* London: Pine Forge Press.

Cutler, D. and Frost, R. (2002) *Taking the Initiative: Promoting Young People's Involvement in Public Decision-Making in the UK.* London: Carnegie Young People Initiative.

Cutler, D. and Taylor, A. (2003) *Expanding and Sustaining Involvement: A Snapshot of Participation Infrastructure for Young People Living in England.* Carnegie UK Trust/Department for Education and Skills.

David, T., Powell, S. and Goouch, K. (2010) 'The world picture', in G. Pugh and B. Duffy (eds) *Contemporary Issues in the Early Years.* London: Sage.

Davis, J.M. (1996) 'Sport for all?', unpublished PhD thesis, University of Edinburgh.

Davis, J.M. (1998) 'Understanding the meanings of children: A reflexive process', *Children & Society,* 12(3): 25–33.

Davis, J.M. (1999) 'Culture, structure and agency in Lothian PE settings', *Scottish Centre Research Papers in Sport, Leisure and Society,* Scottish Centre For Physical Education & Sport, Edinburgh, 3, pp. 1–14.

Davis, J.M. (2000) 'Disability studies as ethnographic research and text: Research strategies and roles for promoting social change?', *Disability and Society,* 15(2): 191–206.

Davis, J.M. (2006) 'Disability, childhood studies and the construction of medical discourses: Questioning attention deficit hyperactivity disorder – a theoretical perspective', in G. Lloyd, J. Stead and D. Cohen (eds) *Critical New Perspectives on ADHD.* London: Taylor and Francis Publishing.

Davis, J.M. (2007) 'Analysing participation and social exclusion with children and young people: Lessons from practice', *International Journal of Children's Rights,* 15(1): 121–46.

Davis, J.M. (2008) *Durham and Darlington Child and Adolescent Mental Health Services Strategy Development Project.* University of Edinburgh/Durham and Darlington Child and Adolescent Mental Health Services.

Davis, J.M. (2009) 'Involving children', in K. Tisdall, J. Davis and M. Gallagher (eds) *Researching with Children and Young People: Research Design, Methods and Analysis*. London: Sage.

Davis, J.M. and Corker, M. (2001) 'Disability studies and anthropology: Difference troubles in academic paradigms', *Anthropology in Action*, 8(2): 18–27.

Davis, J.M. and Hancock, A. (2007) *Early Years Services for Black and Ethnic Minority Families: A Strategy for the Children and Families Department*. Edinburgh: University of Edinburgh/City of Edinburgh Council.

Davis, J.M. and Hogan, J. (2004) 'Research with children: Ethnography, participation, disability, self-empowerment', in C. Barnes and G. Mercer (eds) *Implementing the Social Model of Disability: Theory and Research*. Leeds: The Disability Press.

Davis, J.M. and Watson, N. (2000) 'Disabled children's rights in everyday life: Problematising notions of competency and promoting self-empowerment', *International Journal of Children's Rights*, 8: 211–28.

Davis, J.M. and Watson, N. (2001a) 'Where are the children's experiences? Analysing social and cultural exclusion in "special" and "mainstream" schools', *Disability and Society*, 16(5): 671–87.

Davis, J.M. and Watson, N. (2001b) 'Countering stereotypes of disability: Disabled children and resistance', in M. Corker and T. Shakespeare (eds) *Disability and Postmodernity*. London: Continuum.

Davis, J.M., Burns, K. and Hogan, J. (2006) *Communications 2004 Project: Participation and Disabled Children*. Liverpool Children's Fund.

Davis, J.M. and Hughes, A., with Kilgore, J., Whiting, C. and Abbott, J. (2005) *Early Years Workforce Competencies Review*. Edinburgh: City of Edinburgh Council/University of Edinburgh.

Davis, J.M., Watson N., Corker, M. and Shakespeare, T. (2003) 'Reconstructing disabled childhoods and social policy in the UK', in A. Prout and C. Hallet, *Hearing the Voices of Children*. London: Falmer Press.

Davis, J.M., Watson, N. and Cunningham-Burley, S. (2000) 'Learning the lives of disabled children: Developing a reflexive approach', in P. Christiensen and A. James (eds) *Research with Children*. London: Falmer.

Department of Health (DOH) (1999) *National Service Framework for Mental Health: Modern Standards and Service Models*. London: HMO.

Department of Health (DOH) (2002) *Children's Task Force*. London: HMSO (www.doh.gov.uk/childrenstaskforce).

Desforges, C. and Abouchaar, A. (2003) *The Impact of Parental Involvement, Parent Support and Family Education on Pupil Achievement and Adjustment: A Literature Review. Research Report 433*. London: DfES.

De Shazer, S. and Molnar, A. (1987) 'Solution-focused therapy: Toward the identification of therapeutic tasks', *Journal of Marital and Family Therapy*, 13(4): 349–58.

Dickson, J. (2004) 'Indigenous women as agents of change', presentation to the United Nations Permanent Forum on Indigenous Issues Standing Committee, New York, 12 May.

Dillon, J., Statham, J. and Moss, P. (2001) 'The role of the private market in day care provision for children in need', *Social Policy and Administration*, 35(2): 127–44.

Dolan, P. (2006) 'Family support: From description to reflection', in P. Dolan, J. Canavan and J. Pinkerton (eds) *Family Support as Reflective Practice*. London: Jessica Kingsley.

Dolan, P. (2008) 'Social support, social justice and social capital: A tentative theoretical triad for community development', *Community Development* 39(1): 112–19.

Dolan, P. and McGrath, B. (2006) 'Enhancing support for young people in need: Reflections on informal and formal sources of help', in P. Dolan, J. Canavan and H. Pinkerton (eds) *Family Support as Reflective Practice*. London: Jessica Kingsley.

Dorrian, A-M., Tisdall, K. and Hamilton, D. (2001) *Taking the Initiative: Promoting Young People's Participation in Public Decision Making in Scotland*. London: Carnegie Young People Initiative.

Dyck, I. (1999) 'Body troubles: Women, the workplace and negotiations of disabled identity', in R. Butler and H. Parr (eds) *Mind and Body Spaces: Geographies of Illness, Impairment and Disability*. London: Routledge.

Farrier, S., Davis, J.M. and Bruce, A. (2008) *Evaluation of Durham and Darlington PPO*. Durham Constabulary.

Fawcett, M. (2000) 'Early development: Critical perspectives', in M. Boushel, M. Fawcett and J. Selwyn (eds) *Focus on Early Childhood: Principles and Realities*. Oxford: Blackwell.

Fergusson, D.M., Grant, H., Horwood, L.J. and Ridder, E.M. (2006) 'Randomized trial of the Early Start program of home visitation: Parent and family outcomes', *Pediatrics*, 117(3): 781–6.

Figueroa, P. (1993) 'Equality, multiculturism, antiracism and physical education in the National Curriculum', in J. Evans and B. Davies (eds) *Equality, Equity and Physical Education*. London: Falmer.

Fitzgerald, D. and Kay, J. (2008) *Working Together in Children's Services*. London: Routledge/David Fulton.

Foley, P. (2008) 'Skilled work with children', in P. Foley and A. Rixon (eds) *Changing Children's Services: Working and Learning Together*. Bristol: Policy Press.

Fox, A. (2005) 'Bringing it together: The role of the programme manger', in J. Weinberger, C. Pickstone and P. Hannon (eds) *Learning from Sure Start: Working with Young Children and their Families*. Maidenhead: Open University Press.

Frankenberg, R. (2000) 'Re-representing the embodied child: The muted child, the tamed child and the silenced instrument in Jane Campion's *The Piano*', in A. Prout (ed.) *The Body Childhood and Society*. London: Macmillan Press.

Freeman, M. (1996) 'Living by the code: some issues surrounding a code of conduct for the LIS Profession', *New Library World*, 97(1129): 17–21.

Friedson, E. (1983) 'The theory of professions: State of the art', in R. Dingwall and P. Lewis (eds) *The Sociology of the Professions*. London and Basingstoke: Macmillan.

Frost, N. (2001) 'Professionalism, change and the politics of lifelong learning', *Studies in Continuing Education*, 23(1): 5–17.

Frost, N. (2005) *Professionalism, Partnership and Joined Up Thinking*. Dartington: Research in Practice.

Gabriel, J. (1998) *A Preliminary Analysis of Children and Young People's Participation in the Children's Society*. London: TCS.

Gilbert, J. and Bainbridge, L. (2003) 'Canada – interprofessional education and collaboration: Theoretical challenges, practical solutions', in A. Leathard (ed.) *Interprofessional Collaboration: From Policy to Practice in Health and Social Care*. Hove: Brunner-Routledge.

Gilligan, R. (1999) 'Working with social networks: Key Resources in helping children at risk', in M. Hill (ed.) *Effective Ways of Working with Children and their Families*. London: Jessica Kingsley.

Gilligan, R. (2000) 'Family support: Issues and prospects', in J. Canavan, P. Dolan and J. Pinkerton (eds) *Family Support: Diversion from Diversity*. London: Jessica Kingsley.

Glenny, G. and Roaf, C. (2008) *Multiprofessional Communication: Making Systems Work for Children*. Maidenhead: Open University Press and McGraw-Hill Education.

Haley, J. (1980) *Leaving Home*. New York: McGraw-Hill.

Hallam, A. (2008) *The Effectiveness of Interventions to Address Health Inequalities in the Early Years: A Review of Relevant Literature*. Edinburgh: The Scottish Government.

Hannon, P., Weinberger, J., Pickstone, C. and Fox, A. (2005) 'Looking to the future', in J. Weinberger, C. Pickstone and P. Hannon (eds) *Learning from Sure Start: Working with Young Children and their Families*. Maidenhead: Open University Press.

Harker, R.M., Dobel-Ober, D., Berridge, D. and Sinclair, R. (2004) 'More than the sum of its parts? Inter-professional working in the education of looked after children', *Children & Society*, 18(3): 179–93.

Hawker, D. (2010) 'Children's Trusts and early years services: Integration in action', in G. Pugh and B. Duffy (eds) *Contemporary Issues in the Early Years*. London: Sage.

Herbert, M. (2000) 'Children in control', in J. Canavan, P. Dolan and J. Pinkerton (eds) *Family Support: Direction from Diversity*. London: Jessica Kingsley.

Hill, M. (2005) 'Children's boundaries', in L. McKie and S. Cunningham-Burley (eds) *Families in Society: Boundaries and Relationships*. Bristol: The Policy Press.

Hogan, J. (2002) 'Rhetoric or reality', MA thesis, University of Liverpool.

Hogan, J. (2003) *Liverpool Children's Fund Participation Standards*. Liverpool Children's Fund/City Council.

Honneth, A. (2000) *Suffering from Indeterminacy: An Attempt at a Reactualisation of Hegel's Philosophy of Right, Two Lectures*. Assen: Van Gorcum.

Huxham, C. and Macdonald, D. (1992) 'Introducing collaborative advantage: Achieving inter-organisational effectiveness through meta-strategy', *Management Decision*, 30(3): 50–6.

Hyland, S. (1997) *Will Adults Really Let Us?* The Children's Society/Manchester University.

Jack, G. (2006) 'The area and community components of children's well-being', *Children & Society*, 20(5): 334–47.

James, A. and Prout, A. (1990) 'Contemporary issues in the sociological study of childhood', in A. James and A. Prout (eds) *Constructing and Reconstructing Childhood*. London: Falmer.

James, A. and Prout, A. (1995) 'Hierarchy, boundary and agency', *Sociological Studies in Children*, 7: 77–99.

James, A., Jenks, C. and Prout, A. (1998) *Theorising Childhood*. Cambridge: Polity Press.

Jeffrey, L. (2003) 'Moving on from Child Protection: Messages from research and re-focusing', in N. Frost, A. Lloyd and L. Jeffrey (eds) *The RHP Companion to Family Support*. Lyme Regis: Russell House Publishing.

Jones, C. and Leverett, S. (2008) 'Policy into practice: Assessment, evaluation and multi-agency working with children', in P. Foley and A. Rixon (eds) *Changing Children's Services: Working and Learning Together*. Bristol: Policy Press.

Kasnitz, D. and Shuttleworth, R.P. (1999) 'Engaging anthropology in disability studies', *Position Papers in Disability Studies* 1(1): 1–34, May, Oakland, CA: World Institute on Disability.

Katz, I. (1995) 'Approaches to empowerment and participation', in C. Cloke and M. Davies (eds) *Participation and Empowerment in Child Protection*. London: Pitman.

Kendall, L. and Harker, L. (2002) 'A vision for social care', in L. Kendall and L. Harker (eds) *From Welfare to Wellbeing*. London: Institute for Public Policy Research.

Kennedy, J. and Everest, A. (1991) 'Putting diversity into context', *Personnel Journal*, September: 50–4.

Kirby, P. (1999) *Involving Young Researchers*. York: JRF.

Kirby, P. and Bryson, S. (2002) *Measuring the Magic? Evaluating Young People's Participation in Public Decision-Making*. London: Carnegie Young People Initiative.

Kirby, P., Lanyon, C., Cronin, K. and Sinclair, R. (2003) *Building a Culture of Participation: Involving Young People in Policy, Service Planning, Delivery and Evaluation: Research Report*. Nottingham: DfES.

Kjorholt, A. (2002) 'Small is powerful: Discourses on children and participation in Norway', *Childhood*, 1: 63–82.

Lansdown, G. (2001) *Promoting Children's Participation in Democratic Decision Making*. Florence: UNICEF.

Larson, M.S. (1997) *The Rise of Professionalism*. Berkeley, CA: University of California Press.

Leadbetter, J., Daniels, H.R.J., Edwards, A., Martin, D.M., Middleton, D., Popova, A., Warmington, P.C., Apostol, A. and Brown, S. (2007) 'Professional learning within multi-agency children's services: Researching into practice', *Educational Research*, 49(1): 83–98.

Leathard, A. (2003a) 'Models for interprofessional collaboration', in A. Leathard (ed.) *Interprofessional Collaboration: From Policy to Practice in Health and Social Care*. Hove: Brunner-Routledge.

Leathard, A. (2003b) 'Introduction', in A. Leathard (ed.) *Interprofessional Collaboration: From Policy to Practice in Health and Social Care*. Hove: Brunner-Routledge.

Levitas, R. (1998) *The Inclusive Society? Social Exclusion and New Labour*. London: Macmillan.

Lloyd, G., Stead, J. and Kendrick, A. (2001) *Hang on in There: A Study of Inter-Agency Work to Prevent School Exclusion in Three Local Authorities*. London: National Children's Bureau.

Macdonald, K.M. (1995) *The Sociology of the Professions*. London: Sage.

McGhee, J. and Waterhouse, L. (2002) 'Family support and the Scottish Hearing system', *Child and Family Social Work*, 7: 273–83.

Madanes, C. (1981) *Strategic Family Therapy*. San Francisco, CA: Jossey-Bass.

Malin, N. and Morrow, G. (2007) 'Models of interprofessional working within a Sure Start "Trailblazer" programme', *Journal of Interprofessional Care*, 21(4): 445–57.

Marcus, G. (1986) 'Contemporary problems of ethnography in a world system', in G.E. Marcus and J. Clifford (eds) *Writing Culture: The Poetics and Politics of Ethnography*. Berkeley, CA: University of California Press.

Marcus, G. and Fischer, M. (1986) *Anthropology as a Cultural Critique*. Chicago, IL: Chicago University Press.

Marks, E. (1994) 'Case management in service integration: A concept paper', National Centre for Children in Poverty, Columbia School of Public Health, Columbia.

Mayall, B. (1994) *Negotiating Health: Children at Home and Primary School*. London: Continuum.

Mayall, B. (1996) *Children, Health and the Social Order*. Buckingham: Open University Press.

Mayall, B. (1998) 'Towards a sociology of child health', *Sociology of Health and Illness*, 20: 269–88.

Mayall, B. (2000) 'Conversations with children: Working with generational issues', in P. Christensen and A. James (eds) *Research with Children*. London: Falmer.

Miller, G. and De Shazer, S. (2000) 'Emotions in solution-focused therapy: A re-examination', *Family Process* 39: 5–23.

Milne, V. (2005) 'Joined up working in the Scottish Executive', Research Findings No. 17. Office of Chief Researcher, Scottish Executive, Edinburgh.

Mitchell, L. and Hodgen, E. (2008) *Locality-based Evaluation of Pathways to the Future: Ngā Huarahi Arataki – Stage One Report*. Wellington, NZ: Ministry of Education.

Monk, J. and Frankenberg, R. (1995) 'Being ill and being me: Self, body, and time in multiple sclerosis narratives', in B. Ingstad and S.R. Whyte (eds) *Disability and Culture*. Berkeley, CA: University of California Press.

Moore, S., Tulk, W. and Mitchell, R. (2005) 'Qallunaat crossing: The southern–northern divide and promising practices for Canada's Inuit young people', *First Peoples Child & Family Review*, 2(1): 117–29.

Morris, J. (1992) 'Personal and political: A feminist perspective in researching physical disability', *Disability, Handicap & Society*, 7(2): 157–66.

Morrow, V. (1999) 'Conceptualising social capital in relation to the well-being of children and young people: A critical review', *The Sociological Review*, 47(4): 744–65.

Morrow, V. (2000) '"Dirty Looks" and "Trampy Places" in young people's accounts of community and neighbourhood: Implications for health inequalities', *Critical Public Health*, 10: 141–52.

Morrow, V. and Richards, M. (1996) 'The ethics of social research with children: An overview', *Children & Society*, 10: 28–40.

Moss, P. and Bennett, J. (2006) *Toward a New Pedagogical Meeting Place? Bringing Early Childhood into the Education System*. Briefing Paper for a Nuffield Educational Seminar, September.

Moss, P. and Petrie, P. (2002) *From Children's Services to Children's Spaces*. London: Taylor and Francis.

Nayak, A. (2009) 'Race, ethnicity and young people', in H. Montgomery and M. Kellet (eds) *Children and Young People's Worlds: Developing Frameworks for Integrated Practice*. Bristol: Policy Press.

Newman, T. (2002) '"Young carers" and disabled parents: Time for a change of direction?' *Disability & Society*, 16(6): 613–25.

Nutbrown, C. (1994) 'Teachers and young children in educational establishments', in T. David (ed.) *Working Together for Children*. London: Routledge.

OECD (2001) *Starting Strong I: Early Childhood Education and Care*. Paris: OECD.

OECD (2006) *Starting Strong II: Early Childhood Education and Care*. Paris: OECD.

Owen, S. and Haynes, G. (2010) 'Training and workforce issues in the early years', in G. Pugh and B. Duffy (eds) *Contemporary Issues in the Early Years*. London: Sage.

Parsons, T. and Bales, R.F. (1955) *Family Socialisation and the Interactive Process*. New York: The Free Press.

Percy-Smith, B. Walsh, D. and Thompson, D. (2001) *Young, Homeless and Socially Excluded: Challenges for Policy and Practice*. Northampton: The SOLAR Centre, University College Northampton/The Children's Society.

Piaget, J. (1968) *Six Psychological Studies*. New York: Vintage.

Piaget, J. (1975) *The Moral Judgement of the Child*. London: Routledge.

Priestley, M. (1998) 'Childhood disability and disabled childhoods: Agendas for research', *Childhood*, 5: 207–23.

Prout, A. (2000) 'Children's participation: Control and self-realisation in British late modernity', *Children & Society*, 14: 304–16.

Prout, A., Symmonds, R. and Birchall, J. (2006) 'Reconnecting and extending the research agenda on children's participation: Mutual incentives and the participation chain', in K. Tisdall, J. Davis, M. Hill, and A. Prout (eds) *Children, Childhood and Social Inclusion*. London: Policy Press.

Pugh, G. (2010) 'The policy agenda for early childhood services', in G. Pugh, and B. Duffy (eds) *Contemporary Issues in the Early Years*. London: Sage.

Putnam, R., Leonardi, R. and Nanetti, R. (1993) *Making Democracy Work: Civic Traditions in Modern Italy*. Princeton, NJ: Princeton University Press.

Quality Assurance Agency Scotland (QAAS) (2007) *The Standard for Childhood Practice: Subject Benchmark Statement*. Mansfield: The Quality Assurance Agency for Higher Education.

Read, J., Clements, L. and Rubbain, D. (2006) *Disabled Children and The Law*. London: Jessica Kingsley.

Reeves, S. and Freeth, D. (2003) 'New forms of technology, new forms of collaboration', in A. Leathard (ed.) *Interprofessional Collaboration: From Policy to Practice in Health and Social Care*. Hove: Brunner-Routledge.

Roaf, C. (2002) *Coordinating Services for Included Children: Joined-Up Action*. Basingstoke: Open University Press.

Robinson, J. (1997) 'Listening to disabled youth', *Child Right*, 140: 546–7.

Ross, D. and Ross, S. (1984) 'The importance of the type of question', *Pain*, 19: 71–9.

Rowe, A. (2005) 'The impact of Sure Start on health visiting', in J. Weinberger, C. Pickstone and P. Hannon (eds) *Learning from Sure Start: Working with Young Children and their Families*. Maidenhead: Open University Press.

Riddell, S. and Tett, L. (2001) *Education, Social Justice and Inter-agency Working: Joined-up or Fractured Policy*. London: Routledge.

Ridge, T. (2002) *Childhood Poverty and Social Exclusion: From A Child's Perspective*. Bristol: Policy Press.

Rixon, A. (2008a) 'Working with change', in P. Foley and A. Rixon (eds) *Changing Children's Services: Working and Learning Together*. Bristol: Policy Press.

Rixon, A. (2008b) 'Positive practice relationships', in P. Foley and S. Leverett (eds) *Connecting with Children: Developing Working Relationships*. Bristol: Policy Press.

Rudge, C. (2010) 'Children's Centres', in G. Pugh and B. Duffy (eds) *Contemporary Issues in the Early Years*. London: Sage.

Rugland, W. (1993) 'Assuming the mantle of professionalism', Vaulation Actuary Symposium, USA.

Rutter, M. (2007) 'Sure Start local programmes: An outsider's perspective', in J. Belsky, J. Barnes and E. Melhuish (eds) *The National Evaluation of Sure Start: Does Area-Based Early Intervention Work?* Bristol: Policy Press.

Scott, F. (2006) 'The representation of integration in guidance and documents relating to children's services plans', MSc Childhood Studies thesis, University of Edinburgh, Graduate School of Social & Political Studies.

Seebohm, F. (1989) *Seebohm Twenty Years On: Three Stages in the Development of the Personal Social Services*. London: Policy Studies Institute.

Seidman, S. (1998) 'Are we all in the closet? Notes towards a sociological and cultural turn in queer theory', *European Journal of Cultural Studies*, 1: 177–92.

Selvini, M., Boscolo, L., Checchin, G. and Prata, G. (1978) *Paradox and Counter-Paradox*. New York: J. Aronson.

Shakespeare, T. and Watson, N. (1998) 'Theoretical principles in disabled childhood', in K. Stalker and C. Robinson (eds) *Growing up with Disability*. London: Jessica Kingsley.

Shier, H. (2001) 'Pathways to participation: Openings, opportunities and obligations: A new model for enhancing children's participation in decision-making, in line with article 12.1 of the United Nations Convention on the Rights of the Child', *Children & Society*, 15(2): 107–17.

Shulruf, B. (2009) 'Policy analysis of New Zealand's 10-year strategic plan for early childhood education, Pathways to the Future: Ngā Huarahi Arataki 2002–2012', *Child Health And Education*, 1(3): 162–82.

Sims, D., Fineman, S. and Gabriel, Y. (1993) *Organising and Organisations: An Introduction*. London: Sage.

Sinclair, R. and Franklin, A. (2000) *A Quality Protects Briefing: Young People's Participation*. London: Department of Health.

Siraj-Blatchford, I. (2010) 'Diversity, inclusion and learning in the early years', in G. Pugh and B. Duffy (eds) *Contemporary Issues in the Early Years*. London: Sage.

Smith, A.B., Grima, G., Gaffney, M. and Powell, K. (2000) *Early Childhood Education: Literature Review Report to the Ministry of Education*. Dunedin, NZ: University of Otago, Children's Issues Centre.

Smith, M. (2007) *What is Family Support Work? A Case Study Within the Context of One Local Authority in Scotland*, University of Edinburgh.

Smith, M. and Davis, J.M. (2010) 'Constructions of family support: Lessons from the field', *Administration (Journal of the Institute of Public Administration: Ireland)*, 58.

Stables, J. and Smith, F. (1999) 'Caught in the Cinderella trap: Narratives of disabled parents and carers', in R. Butler and H. Parr (eds) *Mind and Body Spaces: Geographies of Illness, Impairment and Disability*. London: Routledge.

Stainton-Rogers, W. (2001) 'Constructing childhood, constructing child concern', in P. Foley, J. Roche and S. Tucker (eds) *Children in Society*. Basingstoke: Palgrave (in association with the Open University).

Stone, B. and Rixon, A. (2008) 'Towards integrated working', in P. Foley and A. Rixon (eds) *Changing Children's Services: Working and Learning Together*. Bristol: Policy Press.

Swain, J. (1993) 'Taught helplessness? Or a say for disabled students in schools', in J. Swain, V. Finkelstein, S. French and M. Oliver (eds) *Disabling Barriers – Enabling Environments*. London: Sage.

Swain, J. et al. (2004) *North Washington Sure Start Evaluation*. Newcastle: Northumbria University.

Sylva, K., Melhuish, E., Sammons, P., Siraj-Blatchford, I. and Taggert, B. (2004) *The Final Report: Effective Preschool Education. Technical Paper 12*. London: Institute of Education, University of London.

The Children's Society (TCS) (2000) *The Children and Young People's Participation Initiative*. London: TCS.

Tisdall, E.K.M. (1997) *The Children (Scotland) Act 1995: Developing Policy and Law for Scotland's Children*. Edinburgh: TSO.

Tisdall, E. and Davis, J. (2004) 'Making a difference? Bringing children's and young people's views into policy-making', *Children & Society*, April 18(2): 77–96.

Tisdall, E.K.M., Davis, J.M. and Gallagher, M. (2008) 'Reflecting upon children and young people's participation in the UK', *'International Journal of Children's Rights'*, Special Issue, 16: 343–54.

Tisdall, E.K.M., Davis, J.M. and Gallagher, M.J. (eds) (2009) *Research with Children and Young People*. London: Sage.

Tomlinson, K. (2003) *Effective Inter-Agency Working: A Review of the Literature and Examples from Practice*. Slough: NFER.

Toren, C. (2001) 'Learning to know what we feel: What an ontogeny of emotion can tell us about being human', Children in their Places Conference, Brunel University/RAI, 21–23 June.

UPIAS/Disability Alliance (1976) *Fundamental Principles of Disability*. London: Methuen.

Valentine, G. (1999) 'What it means to be a man: The body, masculinities, disability', in R. Butler and H. Parr (eds) *Mind and Body Spaces: Geographies of Illness, Impairment and Disability*. London: Routledge.

Vernon, A. (1997) 'Reflexivity: The dilemmas of researching from the inside', in C. Barnes and G. Mercer (eds) *Doing Disability Research*. Leeds University: The Disability Press.

Vygotsky, L. (1978) *Mind in Society*. Cambridge, MA: Harvard University Press.

Walker, G. (2008) *Working Together for Children: A Critical Introduction to Multi-Agency Working*. London: Continuum.

Warner, J. (1994) 'Childminders and children', in T. David (ed.) *Working Together for Children*. London: Routledge.

Wates, M. (2003) *Young Carers: Disabled Parents' Perspectives*. Nottingham: Disabled Parents Network.

Webster, D. (2000) *The Impact of Organisational Re-Structuring*. Report for the Children's Society Social Work Division.

Webster-Stratton, C. and Herbert, M. (1994) *Troubled Families – Problem Children: Working With Parents: A Collaborative Process*. Chichester: Wiley and Sons.

Weinberger, J. Pickstone, C. and Hannon, P. (2005) *Learning from Sure Start: Working with Young Children and their Families*. Maidenhead: Open University Press.

Whalley, M. (1994) 'Young children in day nurseries and combined centres run by the Social Services Department', in T. David (ed.) *Working together for Children*. London: Routledge.

Whyte, S.R. (1995) 'Constructing epilepsy: Images and contexts in East Africa', in B. Ingstad and S.R. Whyte (eds) *Disability and Culture*. Berkeley, CA: University of California Press.

Wilson, V. and Pirrie, A. (2000) *Multi-Disciplinary Team Working: Indicators of Good Practice*. Edinburgh: SCRE.

Woodhead, M. and Faulkner, D. (2000) 'Subjects, objects or participants? Dilemmas of psychological research with children', in P. Christensen and A. James (eds) *Research with Children*. London: Falmer Press.

Index

Abouchaar, A. 36
agency based initiatives 15
Alderson, P. 76, 95, 104, 114
  on disabled children 80, 86, 87, 88
Aldgate, J. 22, 23, 55
Aldridge, J. 88
Aldridge, M. 18
Anning, A. 3, 31, 111, 118, 126
  on integrated working 14, 17, 18, 19, 20,
    21, 22
anthropology 122
anti-discriminatory practices 51
Asad, T. 122
assessment scales, mental health 63
attachment theories 111
Aubrey, C. 34, 36, 38, 39, 40, 41
Avery, D. 86

Badham, B. 24, 102, 103, 105
Bainbridge, L. 3, 16, 19
balancing of services 22–3
Bales, R.F. 112
Ball, J. 5, 53, 54, 113
Banks, S. 18
Barnes, J. 4, 33, 35, 39
Becker, S. 88
behaviour of children, interpreting 63
Bennett, J. 32, 35, 110
Beresford, B. 80, 81, 88
Berg, I.K. 118
Bertram, T. 2, 14, 15, 16, 17, 18, 21
bilingualism 46
Billingham, K. 4, 33, 35, 39
black and ethnic minority families 43, 44, 45,
    47, 51, 56
Blackburn, C. 38, 39
Borland, M. 74, 102
Bourdieu, P. 117
Bowlby, J. 111
Bricher, G. 87
Brighton, Children's Centres in 33, 34
Broadhead, P. 16, 55, 117
Bronfenbrenner, U. 6, 23, 76, 116
Brooker, L. 5, 50
Brown, M. 35, 41
Bruce, T. 4, 110, 111, 118
Bryson, S. 73, 74, 103, 104
budgeting, participatory 100–1
bullying, racist 48
Burman, E. 112
Burns, K. 79

Cain, M. 57
Cairns, L. 24, 91, 98, 104, 107, 125
CAMHS *see* Child and Adolescent Mental
    Health Services (CAMHS)
Canada 5, 53, 55
centres, integrated 16, 27, 30, 41
  in Brighton 33, 34
  heads of 39
  see also Children's Centres
Chaskin, R.J. 53, 54, 113
Cheung, M. 54
child agency concept, critique 124
Child and Adolescent Mental Health Services
    (CAMHS) 6, 63, 117
  consultation and participation involving
    young people 69–74
  contradictory constructions of young
    people 67–9
  defining mental health needs and support
    concepts 75–8
  Durham and Darlington, summary report
    57–78
    achievements of first strategy 60–2
    commissioning group, role 70–1
    integrated strategy evaluation 59–62
    key findings 60
    prevalence of mental health issues,
      estimating 62–4
    strategic issues 58
    ecological and individualised approaches
      76–7
    multi-agency approaches 64–7, 69, 77
    politically nuanced holistic models 77–8
    tiers of services 65, 78
child carers 89
child protection 22, 111
child-centred perspective 3, 23
childhood theories 4, 23, 109, 111–12, 118,
    122–8
Children's Centres 30, 33, 34, 41, 55
Christensen, P. 78, 123
Christie, D. 2, 13, 16
circle time 67–8
Clark, M. 5, 32, 35, 50
Clarke, J. 34
Cockburn, T. 104, 105
cognitive behavioural therapy (CBT) 67–8, 69
Cohen, B. 2, 4, 31, 110
  on co-location, roles and professional
    training 32, 34, 35, 40, 41
  on integrated working 16, 20, 21, 22

DIVERSITY, EQUALITY AND ACHIEVEMENT IN EDUCATION

Gianna Knowles and **Vini Lander** both at *University of Chichester*

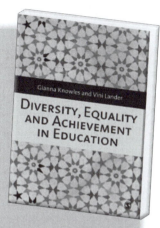

Most classrooms contain children from a variety of backgrounds, where home culture, religious beliefs and the family's economic situation all impact on achievement. This needs to be recognised by teachers in order to establish fair, respectful, trusting and constructive relationships with children and their families, which will allow every child to reach their full potential.

This book looks at real issues that affect teachers in the classroom, and examines a variety of influences affecting child development. It provides you with the theoretical and practical information you need to ensure you understand the complex factors which affect the children in your care, and it encourages good, thoughtful teaching. Dealing with some of the less widely addressed aspects of diversity and inclusion, the book considers:

- children who are asylum seekers
- the notion of 'pupil voice'
- what diversity and equality mean in practice
- gender and achievement
- looked-after children
- social class
- disability
- ethnicity and whiteness

This book is essential reading for any education student looking at diversity and inclusion, and for teachers in role looking for advice on how to meet the professional standards.

February 2011 • 192 pages
Cloth (978-1-84920-600-6) • £65.00
Paper (978-1-84920-601-3) • £21.99

ALSO FROM SAGE

CONTEMPORARY ISSUES IN LEARNING AND TEACHING

Edited by **Margery McMahon**, **Christine Forde** and **Margaret Martin** all at *University of Glasgow*

Contemporary Issues in Learning and Teaching looks at current issues across the three key areas of policy, learning and practice. It will help you to think critically on your Education course, and to make connections between the processes of learning and the practicalities of teaching. The book addresses key issues in primary, secondary and special education, and includes examples from all four countries of the UK.

The contributors reflect on current thinking and policy surrounding learning and teaching, and what it means to be a teacher today. Looking at the practice of teaching in a wider context allows you to explore some of the issues you will face, and the evolving expectations of your role in a policy-led environment. The book focuses on core areas of debate including:

- education across different contexts and settings
- teaching in an inclusive environment
- Continuing Professional Development (CPD) for practitioners

Each chapter follows the same accessible format. They contain case studies and vignettes providing examples and scenarios for discussion; introduction and summary boxes listing key issues and concepts explored in the chapter; key questions for discussion reflection; and further reading.

This essential text will be ideal for undergraduate and postgraduate courses, including BEd//BA degrees, initial teacher-training courses, and Masters in Education programmes.

All editors and contributors are based in the Faculty of Education at Glasgow University, UK.

November 2010 • 232 pages
Cloth (978-1-84920-127-8) • £65.00
Paper (978-1-84920-128-5) • £21.99

ALSO FROM SAGE

CHILDREN LEARNING OUTSIDE THE CLASSROOM

From Birth to Eleven

Edited by **Sue Waite** *University of Plymouth*

Learning outside the classroom is increasingly seen as beneficial in both early years and primary settings, and it is becoming embedded in the curriculum, but what are the benefits of this approach? What do children learn from being outside the classroom?

This book explores why learning beyond the classroom is important for children, and offers practical examples of how to improve outdoor learning experiences for all children. In the face of the increasing restriction of children's outdoor experiences, it will help the reader rise to the challenge of finding creative opportunities for working across the curriculum through outdoor activities.

Chapters cover:
• the theory behind learning outside the classroom transition from early years to primary practice
• what outdoor learning looks like, in different contexts
• teaching and learning across the curriculum outdoors
• how to evaluate the effectiveness of different outdoor activities, and learning outside the classroom as a whole.

Each chapter has case studies, thoughts on theory, points for practice and summaries to help readers digest the most important information. Critical thinking and reflective practice are encouraged throughout to support consideration of how outdoor learning relates to the curricula in England, Wales, Scotland and Northern Ireland.

February 2011 • 264 pages
Cloth (978-0-85702-047-5) • £65.00
Paper (978-0-85702-048-2) • £21.99

ALSO FROM SAGE

CHILDREN'S RIGHTS IN PRACTICE

Edited by **Phil Jones** *University of Leeds* and
Gary Walker *Leeds Metropolitan University*

Considering the rights of the child is now central
to all fields involving children and to good multi-
agency working. This book offers an explanation of the theoretical issues and the key policy
developments that are crucial to all professions,
and helps the reader to understand children's
rights in relation to their role in working with children and young people. Looking at education,
health, social care and welfare, it bridges the gap
between policy and practice for children from Birth
to 19 years. Chapters cover:
- the child's right to play
- youth justice, children's rights and the voice of the child
- ethical dilemmas in different contexts
- involvement, participation and decision making
- safeguarding and child protection, social justice and exclusion.

This book helps the reader understand what constitutes good practice, whilst
considering the advantages and tensions involved in working across disciplines
to implement children's rights against a complex legislative and social policy
backdrop.

April 2011 • 256 pages
Cloth (978-1-84920-379-1) • £65.00
Paper (978-1-84920-380-7) • £22.99

ALSO FROM SAGE